MW00999189

ED MITCHELL'S
BARBEQUE

ED MITCHELL'S
BARBEQUE

ecco
An Imprint of HarperCollinsPublishers

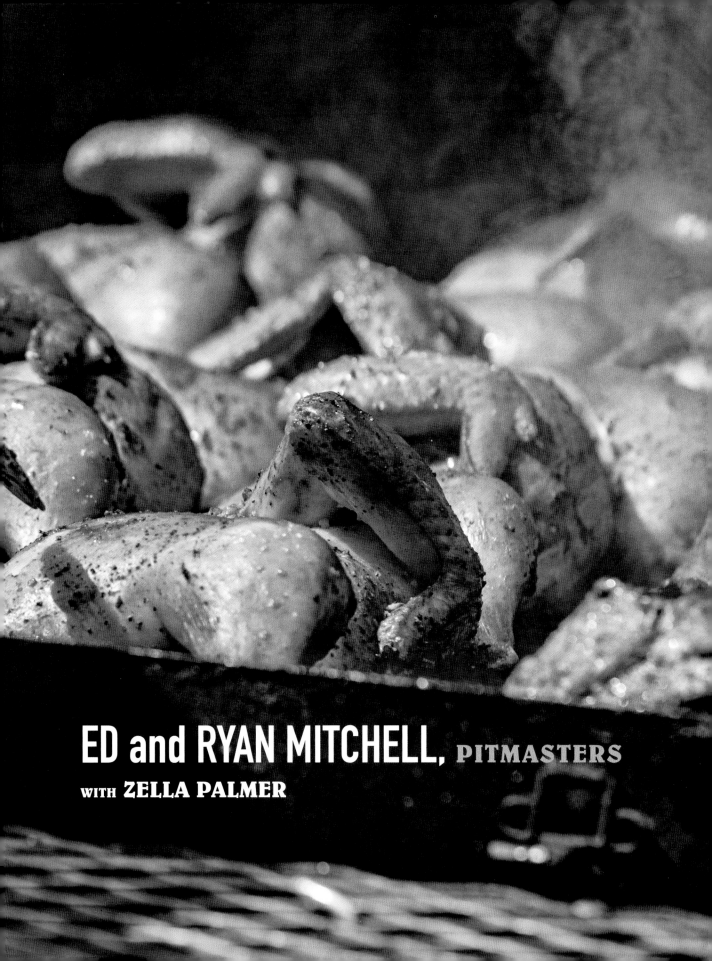

ED and RYAN MITCHELL, *PITMASTERS*

WITH **ZELLA PALMER**

For
LAWYER, BEATRICE, AND
THEODORE SANDARS,
WILLIAM "WILLIE"
MITCHELL, JAMES KIRBY,
SHERI HALL GILBERT,
JOHNNY "JUNE" BRUNSON,
AND ERADER MILLS

HEAVENLY FATHER,
FROM THE ABUNDANCE OF
YOUR STREAMS, FIELDS
AND EARTH YOU HAVE SEEN
FIT TO BLESS OUR TABLE,
AND WE ARE GRATEFUL.
WE PRAY FOR YOUR
CONSTANT GUIDANCE IN
ALL THINGS AND LET US
NEVER FORGET TO GIVE
THANKS FOR YOU
HAVE BLESSED THE HANDS
ON THE COOK.
AMEN.
—NORMA JEAN
AND CAROLE DARDEN,
SPOONBREAD AND
STRAWBERRY WINE

CONTENTS

Generational Wealth: Growing Up in Barbeque

Pit-cooked whole-hog barbeque is the last vestige of Southern barbeque. This technique and approach to pit cooking whole-hog barbeque—or simply "barbeque," as us Carolinians call it—is a rich cultural activity that has overlooked Black people whose forefathers perfected this craft on plantations across the South. Our stories have largely been untold, especially from the likes of Misters Ed and Ryan Mitchell, a family that knows the culture from both a lived and business perspective.

The richness of Mr. Mitchell's story is that he experienced the Jim Crow South and its remnants firsthand when segregation in Wilson, North Carolina, dominated life. Further, his generation is the last to remember working in the tobacco fields. Tobacco-planting culture was part of barbeque culture in towns like Wilson. Men in his era cured tobacco with hardwoods like oak and hickory instead of propane gas. Hence it was nothing to barbeque a hog along a tobacco barn during curing season as the embers were already available. Mr. Mitchell learned to cook barbeque in the ground and in a traditional pit on a farm preserved by Black hands, like his grandfather did.

I know Mr. Mitchell is culturally connected to barbeque because he was given a swig of moonshine, for cooking a hog, a rite of passage and cultural norm

for manhood in the South. Mr. Mitchell is a legend. Mr. Mitchell epitomizes the ideology of picking oneself up by one's bootstraps—his time working at Ford Motor Company, serving in Vietnam, and then returning to Wilson to help his beloved mother run their family general store. But too many times Black business owners run into unnecessary systematic racism that creates too many obstacles on their journey to pursue the American dream. Mr. Mitchell's life story sheds light on the joy and pain of being Black in America while running a family business

in the rural South on land that his ancestors tilled for free and in bondage.

The Mitchell story continues with his son, Ryan. The dynamics of being raised in rural North Carolina made it a priority for Ryan to pursue higher education. Ryan is part of my generation, sons of Black farmers and pitmasters who carry many degrees and have experience working for corporate America but in their hearts are called back to the land, back to family, to build generational wealth and to live out what New Orleans artist Bmike calls our "ancestors' wildest dreams." Ryan worked hard trying to prove himself in finance, creating wealth for shareholders while his dad longed for his son's return. When Ryan was offered a severance package from his corporate finance job, he returned to Wilson to become a shareholder in his family's barbeque business and legacy. Ryan came home like a beautiful prodigal son, equipped with youth, education, business acumen, and drive. Ryan is truly an inspiration for my generation.

Mr. Ed Mitchell, his son, Ryan, and their entire family are on a powerful and compelling journey to build a multigenerational legacy. Their journey is inspiring. They are truly a positive example of a Black father and son running a barbeque business in the rural South who have stayed united in faith and hard work, in spite of any challenges they encountered. The Mitchells were the family to put pit-cooked barbeque on some of the biggest stages, always representing Eastern North Carolina and those that tilled the land and cooked barbeque in the best and worst of times.

As barbeque becomes a big personality in the media and technology evolves, we must never forget what Mr. Mitchell envisioned: traditional whole-hog barbeque cooking; landownership; hard work; authenticity; and lifting up those Black men and women who were erased from barbeque history. This book is dedicated to our ancestors, Wilson, Eastern North Carolina, the Carolinas, and the barbeque community. Mr. Mitchell, I thank you from the bottom of my heart for epitomizing what Black men from the rural South are all about: hard work, ingenuity, integrity, family, and barbeque. We are blessed and honored to read about your barbeque heritage.

—Howard J. Conyers, PhD
BBQ Pitmaster/Rocket Scientist/
Kingsford Mentor, "Preserve the Pit"

The Promise and Threat of Ed Mitchell

I can see Ed Mitchell now, a gray-and-white beard framing his wide face, overalls draping his body, a gimme cap high on his head. Chopping a pit-cooked whole hog into bits of soft flesh and crisp skin, he worked beneath a pop-up tent in a boggy field across the street from my house in Oxford, Mississippi, on an October evening in 2002, receiving congregants like a storefront preacher after service.

Four days later, *New York Times* readers woke to a picture of Ed Mitchell on the front page. In the months and years that followed, his fame spread. He became a recurring headliner at the Big Apple Barbeque Block Party in New York City. When Zingerman's Roadhouse in Ann Arbor, Michigan, added hickory-roasted barbeque to their menu, they brought in Ed Mitchell for a consultation. He competed on camera against Bobby Flay, back when food TV and Flay were at their zenith.

In the early years of the twenty-first century, Mitchell became the go-to guy for writers and eaters like me, in search of whole-hog barbeque and rural authenticity. He had earned college degrees in sociology and public administration and built a career with Ford before returning home. That's a long-winded way of saying that Mitchell did not fit conservative white stereotypes about Black barbeque. That was part of his appeal. Here was part of his threat:

Mitchell was a Black man, working with Black farmers, cooking like his Black forebears, trying to center Black contributions.

On that Saturday, I got to know him. Mitchell was one of seven pitmasters who cooked for the Southern Foodways Alliance Symposium, a three-day exploration of barbeque I helped organize in Oxford, Mississippi. All were talented, though you could tell Mitchell was going to be the star. The barbeque boom, which he helped drive by force of bright personality and hard work, wouldn't gain national traction until the 2010s. But on that day in 2002, in that waterlogged field, Ed Mitchell began a conversation about Black knowledge and labor and barbeque that still reverberates today.

—John T. Edge,
author of *The Potlikker Papers*
and host of *TrueSouth*

In the Country

Today, North Carolina's Piedmont urban centers at Charlotte and the Research Triangle are the drivers of the state's wealth and popular image. In my childhood, though, tobacco was still king, and Coastal Plain towns like Wilson, Goldsboro, and Greenville practically printed money when farmers hauled bright gold cured tobacco leaves to market.

Wilson County was relatively late to the tobacco game. Its county seat, Wilson, was founded in 1849, and the county itself was cobbled together from surrounding counties in 1855. In the early 1700s, with the removal of the Tuscarora after their defeat at nearby Fort Neoheroka, English settlers in Virginia pushed into the area, accompanied by enslaved Africans. In the early 1800s, a trading settlement called Toisnot and the village of Hickory Grove developed at what is now the city of Wilson. In 1840, the Wilmington and Weldon Railroad linked the area south to North Carolina ports and north to markets in Virginia, greatly expanding the local economy.

Though Wilson County was not home to large plantations with white-columned big houses, slaveholders dominated the county's wealth and governance. The labor of enslaved African Americans was vital to the economy. By 1860, enslaved persons comprised just under 40 percent of Wilson County's population, two-thirds living roughly

east of present-day US Highway 301 near today's rural villages of Black Creek, Stantonsburg, and Saratoga. They raised cotton and food crops and cared for their enslavers' livestock, of which hogs were most numerous. Salt pork and fatback were staples of the diets of the enslaved, and the end of harvest season and the coming of cold weather meant hog-killing time—and barbeque.

For most African Americans in Wilson County, little changed after emancipation. Freed from slavery, they remained yoked to grueling agricultural work, often on the same farms on which they had labored as enslaved people. Many went north and west seeking greener pastures, literal and metaphorical. One such migrant was the boy who would become Dr. Joseph H. Ward of Indianapolis, hospital founder, personal physician to Madam C. J. Walker, and great-grandfather to Zella Palmer.

The 1890s, however, ushered in a new world. The first bright-leaf tobacco markets opened, followed by manufacturing plants, and the Norfolk Southern Railway connected the town

west to North Carolina's commerce centers. Tobacco processing plants—stemmeries, prizeries, warehouses, and cigarette factories—drew African American migrants to Wilson from across Eastern North Carolina and as far south as Georgia. Farm laborers threw down their hoes and moved to town, seeking steadier work and greater freedom. Several Black neighborhoods sprang up, most east of the Atlantic Coast Line Railroad tracks, and a tiny Black business district emerged. Churches, fraternal organizations, and civic and social clubs anchored a solid working-class community. Samuel H. Vick led the political and economic vanguard of East Wilson, platting new neighborhoods, cofounding a Black bank and hospital, and welcoming Booker T. Washington to town.

I was born in that Black hospital in Wilson at the tail end of this deeply segregated world. My parents were committed to seizing for my sister and me all the privileges they had been denied, but also to maintaining our connections to the community. My local family was quite small, but my cousins' father came from a big family with deep Wilson County roots. Their grandmother had nearly a dozen siblings, whom we also called "aunt" and "uncle," and we were always invited to Barnes family gatherings. Easter, Thanksgiving, and Christmas dinners rotated among the aunts' houses, and we squeezed in with the rest at tables groaning with turkey, sliced ham, greens, candied yams, and giblet gravy studded with chopped boiled eggs.

The highlight of the family culinary circuit was the annual Fourth of July family reunion at Aunt Minnie's out "in the country." Aunt Minnie and Uncle Thomas were tenant farmers who rented the large two-story white house at which they hosted those reunions. (Much later I realized this house had been built by an enslaver, and still later realized that Zella's maternal ancestors had been enslaved there!) Many of the cars wedged onto the front lawn bore New York and New Jersey license plates— Wilson County's diaspora returned. Aunt Minnie; her sisters Edie Bell, Pet, Alice, and Lula; and their daughters

and daughters-in-law commanded the kitchen, and platter after platter of homegrown, home-cooked goodness emerged onto tables on the screened-in side porch. Outside toward the barn, chickens strutting, my cousins' uncles tended an earthen pit in which a split pig lay splayed over a rack, juices popping and spitting. Off to the side, jugs filled to the brim with the family's special vinegar-and-red-pepper sauce awaited.

Of course, we didn't have to wait for a pig pickin' to eat barbeque in Wilson. Parker's Barbeque was nearly twenty years old by the time I was born, and Godwin's, which operated out of a storefront downtown, was even older. They were white-owned establishments, and we had complicated relationships with them. Though integration had finally firmly arrived in Wilson, no Black people I knew entered Parker's dining room. Instead, as African Americans had done since the place opened in 1946, we went around back to the takeout entrance to pick up white paper bags stuffed with barbeque, fried chicken, slaw, and corn sticks. At Godwin's, my favorite, we did

take seats in the well-worn booths inside, but my father plainly remembered that in the not-so-distant days past he would not have been allowed in, and he seldom thoroughly enjoyed his meal.

I left Wilson for college in the early 1980s. Visits home always included a stop at Parker's, and eventually, we ventured into the dining room. By the mid-1990s, I was living in Atlanta, and visits to Wilson had a new destination—Mitchell's on 301, not far from my parents' house. My father was so pleased to support a Black-owned barbeque business, especially his friend Ed's, and was not the least bit surprised when I called home to crow, "Mr. Mitchell's in the *New York Times!*"

Six years ago, I began curating *Black Wide-Awake*, a blog dedicated to the African American history, families, and culture of Wilson. I was born during a cusp in my community's history, in that transition between the worlds of segregation and integration, and feel both well situated and compelled to carry the past forward. My research has been omnivorous, but I've kept a special eye out for evidence of the history of Wilson's food culture. I've uncovered stories of Saturday-night barbeque stands tended by fiddling farmhands; the all-Black volunteer fire brigade, Red Hot Hose Company's famous barbeque New Year's celebrations; World War I–era barbeque fundraisers for the hospital in which I was born a half century later; a woman-owned café serving pit-cooked barbeque in the Black business block; and barbeque laid out for family reunions and funeral repasts. I've also seen references to barbeque being prepared by "help" or "under supervision" at whites-only establishments like Sutton's, the Dixie Inn, the Zam Zam Club, and Silver Lake Park.

So, who was doing all this cooking?

The names of Wilson's historic barbeque masters, the so-called pitboys of the nineteenth and twentieth centuries, are largely forgotten, and their craft is dying. The heirs to their tradition not only must preserve and pass down their foodways, they must also be griots. Ed and Ryan Mitchell have taken up both mantles. In the spirit of sankofa, they have gone back for what we almost lost, so that our children and our children's children can keep it going.

—Lisa Y. Henderson, Esq.

Where There Is Flavor, There Is History

BENEVOLENT ANCESTORS,
GUIDE US ON THIS
BARBEQUE JOURNEY
TO TELL ED MITCHELL'S
STORY.
    WE OFFER LIBATIONS
AND PRAISE.

Where there is flavor, there is history. For years, my mother and grandmother told me stories about their roots in Eastern North Carolina and how my family migrated to Indianapolis, Indiana. From my grandmother Mary's rocking chair, I listened intently to memories of her parents and watched her journal her life in dime-store notebooks, praying that the next generation would treasure the hard work, journey, and sacrifice she and her generation had made to exist and survive. Tears would stream down her face as I watched her delicate hand swirl beautiful cursive letters over the fading lined paper.

As a child, I didn't understand that grief is everlasting when you lose the parents who nurtured and raised you. After my grandmother's death, my mother was the last one to know their stories. On our kitchen bookshelf, she cherished *Spoonbread and Strawberry Wine: Recipes and Reminiscences of a Family* by Norma Jean and Carole Darden, two sisters with deep roots in Wilson, North Carolina, similar to our family. At ten years old,

I would sit at the kitchen table thumbing through the Darden sisters' cookbook. "Aren't they beautiful? They are from my grandfather's hometown," Mommy said, and smiled softly as she continued to tell stories of how we got over.

Verdant North Carolina, where my matriarchal last names of Ward, Hagans, and Locklear have grown many branches. My mother was so happy to share stories of her grandparents with my sons and take them to Parker's Barbecue in Wilson. This was the best classroom they could ever have, to stand where our ancestors once stood, to eat what they ate. In 2019, we took our family vacation to North Carolina; it would be the last while my dad was alive. I will cherish that family trip forever.

In 2020, like many of you, I was quarantined at home in New Orleans, worried about my parents as they sheltered in our family home in Chicago. One morning, I checked my work email and there was a request to meet with Ed and Ryan Mitchell, legendary father-and-son barbeque pitmasters from Wilson, North Carolina. My cousin Lisa, a native Wilsonite, drove from Atlanta for a masked porch visit to check on me. I told Lisa about the email I'd received. "Zella, please tell them that you have

roots in Wilson when they interview you to write their cookbook," she said. After she returned to Atlanta, I scheduled the interview with the Mitchells, and sure enough, I told them about my matriarchal roots in Wilson.

And so the journey returned back to Wilson, to four generations of the Mitchell family. Immediately, I was enamored of and humbled to meet Ed Mitchell, the legend, the "pitmaster." I felt like a kid meeting Black Santa Claus for the first time, because Black Santa always knew your people. We visited neighbors, friends, family, and neighborhood historians and ate together as he shared pieces of his life and his love for family and Eastern North Carolina Barbeque. We walked through the now-closed Mitchell's Ribs, Bar-B-Q & Chicken on Ward Boulevard, where he built a dream from his parents' small grocery store. I stood in their commercial kitchen, astounded by the pits he had engineered with perfect airflow. I waited patiently for the day when he would let me try Ed Mitchell's old-fashioned whole-hog barbeque.

The Mitchells invited me to attend the Pinehurst Barbecue Festival at Pinehurst Resort, founded in 1895. "Sit next to me, baby," said Ed, and I did, watching the magic, the well-orchestrated symphony of Ed Mitchell; his brothers,

Stevie and Aubrey; his beloved son, Ryan; and his nephew A. J. as they laid the coals on the old-school grill as if building the pyramids. Ed Mitchell gave direction as an all-star football coach. "That's what I'm talking about," he said as he taste tested a masterpiece in the making. He fixed me a plate of fresh golden glistening cracklin' with chopped barbeque and finely shredded slaw with the perfect balance of vinegar and seasoning. Nothing could prepare me for the moment I bit into Ed Mitchell's whole-hog barbeque. I wasn't the only one who was blown away; a line almost two streets long had formed. I heard someone call out, "I drove for miles to get some of your barbeque, Ed. I can't wait." I watched as eyes rolled and heads shook after each glorious bite. A woman who'd had too many beers came up to Ed Mitchell, leaned over him— unmasked, during COVID—and said, "You are the first Black man to make me feel this way." I nearly fell out of my chair. I asked him, "Does that happen often?" He laughed jovially. "Baby, you don't know the half of it."

What struck me most was our initial conversations when the Mitchells talked about Mother Doretha Mitchell, the nucleus, the conductor, and the oracle of the family, with so much love and adoration. At ninety-one years old, she still leads the family with grace and unwavering faith. I was elated, anticipating our first meeting after hearing so many stories about her from all the men in the Mitchell family. Upon entering Mother Doretha's intimate home, where she had loved and raised three sons and her grandson, Ryan, with her soulmate and husband, Willie Mitchell, the alluring scent of every dish she prepared for our lunch and the presence of the Holy Spirit drew me in.

One of my favorite Bible scriptures adorned the walls: "You will be blessed when you come in and blessed when you go out" (Deuteronomy 28:6). I knew at that moment that she was everything the Mitchells described her to be. Walking into the kitchen, I saw there were mounds of fried freshly caught fish and shrimp laid delicately on large platters next to buttery, crispy sweet potato jacks, and Ed Mitchell looked at me with a firstborn son's pride. "You ready to try Mother Doretha's trotters? It will hurt you, baby." The inner child in me was jumping up and down, ready for a life-changing meal—and a life-changing meal it was. We all sat at Mother Doretha's elegantly dressed table waiting for her to bless our food and to bless us. At that moment, I thanked God for having the honor to sit at their table and tell their story. Their story changed me, and I know this cookbook will change you.

The Mitchells wanted to tell their story on their own terms and for the images to speak for themselves. For too long, Black folks in the culinary world took their stories and recipes to the grave or told their stories through filtered second-party lenses that had their own opinions of who is deserving of the spotlight or whose truth is valid. To be seen is to be heard. Each recipe tells the Mitchells' story over four generations rooted in Wilson, a small town that was once the capital of tobacco production in the United States. Where faith, family, farming, and whole-hog barbeque runs through bloodlines.

When we started this project, I called a dear friend, Chef Andrea Reusing of Lantern Restaurant in Chapel Hill, North Carolina, for her to recommend a top food photographer in North Carolina. "Easy—Baxter Miller." At Baxter and her partner Ryan's home and work studio in New Bern, North Carolina, we all reimagined the legacy of the Eastern North Carolina whole-hog barbeque and family-staple dishes that the Mitchells and many North Carolinians share. We were inspired by textiles, color, and patterns that are in alignment with the African American experience and aesthetic. Conversations and questions ensued: Who decides what deserves to be served on a silver platter? Can we share our commonality and heritage through barbeque elegantly displayed not only on silver trays but on dishes made by Jesalyn Keziah, an Indigenous potter and member of the Lumbee Tribe of North Carolina, as we bring barbeque back to its roots, to the land, to the people?

That day we gathered by the river to feast on the fruits of whole-hog barbeque and all of Mother Doretha's cherished dishes. We recognized that food is the gathering, the hands that fire the pits and pass the food around the table; this is the true root of Southern food. Each bite is sacred and is to be preserved so that we remember and honor our ancestors. The collard greens, cornbread, barbeque, and love for labor and family, not the presentation but the ethereal feeling as

we cocked our heads back and smiled at each other as we tasted generations of skill and flavor—that is the essence of Ed Mitchell's renowned barbeque.

I delved into the research, read every barbeque book I could; made calls to colleagues, historians, and barbeque aficionados; interviewed the entire Mitchell family and native Wilsonites. But it wasn't until we visited São Paulo, Brazil, where Ed and Ryan were invited to headline the 2022 Churrascada International Barbecue Festival, that I truly felt the magnitude of Ed Mitchell. He was valued, honored, and admired by so many Brazilian barbeque fans, young and old. At seventy-six years old, he boarded a plane to Brazil determined to fulfill his ancestors' dreams, break boundaries, and pass the torch to the next generation: his treasured son, Ryan Mitchell.

From America's inception, African Americans have always had to adapt and rise above their circumstances, and Ed Mitchell's story is woven into the fabric of American barbeque history.

During a research visit to the Wilson Library Special Collections at UNC-Chapel Hill, I encountered the history of the Barbecue Presbyterian Church, founded in 1758 in Harnett County, North Carolina, by Highland Scot immigrants. A newly arrived Scotswoman stood at the port in Wilmington and saw Black people for the first time. She asked the captain, "Who are they?" He remarked, "Oh, everyone turns black like that after a few months in this climate." As she walked off the dock, she heard Scottish Gaelic, her native tongue, assuming that the two men were fellow Scots only to find out that "their skin was black." She turned around to find a friendly Black woman greeting her with *Ceud mìle fàilte!* The Scotswoman ran back to the dock, demanding that the captain take her back to Scotland, "Immediately, if not sooner!" This story reminds us that the legacy of barbeque in North Carolina was cross-cultural. It broke language barriers and previous cultural norms, and laid the foundation for Ed Mitchell to exist in a world that wasn't always welcoming.

As we returned from Brazil, Ryan shared construction plans of the much-anticipated next chapter in the Mitchell story: the Preserve, their next barbeque restaurant in Raleigh, North Carolina, a renovation of the oldest ale house in North Carolina. During the long plane ride home, I shed tears of joy, resonating in the way Mother Doretha's fervent prayers over her family were realized in her grandbaby Ryan, educated in

economics, who took the family torch and ran hard to get their own unprocessed sugar barbeque sauces and rubs in six thousand stores across the United States and waited patiently to open the Preserve. "I'm not interested in fame," he said. "God put me here to bless my family and North Carolina. I am focused and patient. I won't rest until it's done. I can't be influential and broke. I have to show the next generation another way."

This is the American story of Eastern North Carolina whole-hog barbeque and how Ed Mitchell became a pitmaster with tenacity and faith.

—Zella Palmer

INTRODUCTION

"I Can't Give Up"

LONG AFTER IT WAS
NECESSARY, UNCLE VESS
ATE THE LEAVINGS
OFF THE HOG, DOUSED
THEM WITH VINEGAR
SAUCE.

—Honorée Fanonne
Jeffers, "The Gospel of
Barbeque"

My journey into the barbeque business began with a lunch I made for my mama. It was 1991. I was a forty-five-year-old man grieving the loss of my hero and trying to survive without the patriarch of our family. I hadn't realized my father was as sick as he was. He had terminal cancer, and one night he just slipped away. My mother called me and I came home quickly to be with her. He and Mama had been a team—Black entrepreneurs in a racially divided part of North Carolina. Their grocery store, Mitchell's Supermarket, was filled with everyday goods from penny candy to cooking oil. It was a symbol of African American progress and Black-owned business.

But without my dad there, friends stopped popping by, and business slowed down.

Early that morning, I dropped by the store to check in on Mama. She wasn't herself. Ever since my dad's death, my mom hadn't been as jovial as she used to be. I will never forget when she told me, "I've been here all day and I only sold seventeen dollars in food." I knew I had to step up and take care of my mama as the eldest son in the family. I didn't mind— I've always been a mama's boy. I wanted to make my mother feel better and let her know that she could count on me. So I did what came naturally to us Mitchells: I asked her what she wanted to eat. Mama said, "I have a taste for some good old-fashioned barbeque."

I knew what that meant, so I got my hands on a thirty-five-pound pig— that's a small one. I rolled my parents' rustic cooker into the parking lot of their grocery and fired up the coals.

While the pig cooked, Mama prepared some Eastern North Carolina coleslaw and slowly braised collards. Soon, the smoke filled the air and the pork skin started to crackle. We seasoned and chopped it up on the meat counter in the back, and the fresh barbeque smell permeated the storefront. Our customers, the few we had left, asked, "Y'all selling barbeque now?" Mama looked at me in silence for a moment, then said, "Yes, we are selling barbeque." She fixed the customer a barbeque sandwich. They must have told a few others, because soon we had a line form and all thirty-five pounds of our hog was gone.

That evening, as I was closing up the store, I heard someone shaking the door. Thinking we were about to be robbed, I put on my best James Earl Jones voice to address the intruder. Low and behold, it was a customer from earlier trying to get another barbeque sandwich. I told him, "We don't have any more barbeque but we will have some more tomorrow."

Wilson, North Carolina, is no stranger to barbeque. I would say our small rural town is a founding bedrock to the tradition of whole-hog barbeque and growing tobacco. It's home to two of the largest barbeque joints in the state, Parker's Barbecue and Bill Ellis Barbeque. Parker's claims to serve roughly 20,000 pounds of barbeque weekly. However, with the commercialization of the food industry starting in the 1960s, locals no longer barbequed the traditional way, using natural, farm-raised hogs. Most barbeque restaurants were using store-bought farm-raised pork shoulders, cooked over gas instead of coal fires, and the flavor wasn't the same.

The next day, I bought a slightly larger pig and repeated our whole-hog-barbeque-for-sale experiment. Little by little, our production increased. I put

aside my other hustles and decided to help my mama full-time, building the business with my brothers, Aubrey and Stevie. By the early 1990s, I had transformed Mitchell's Supermarket into Mitchell's Ribs, Chicken & Bar-B-Q. We never looked back.

I had no idea that lunch with Mama would shape the rest of my life—that my family's Eastern North Carolina barbeque would take me around the world to become one of the most internationally recognized barbeque pitmasters. From 2002 until 2018, I was invited year after year to headline the Big Apple Barbecue Block Party in New York City. Famous

food writers like Michael Pollan and Peter Kaminsky, and chefs like Anthony Bourdain and Bobby Flay, traveled to Wilson to learn how Ed Mitchell, Willie and Doretha's son, cooked whole hogs, the traditional way.

I never considered the possibility of making a living as a pitmaster because barbeque was just a way of life for us. We celebrated it through family, church functions, and events. No one I knew who actually owned anything had ever made a career of it. All the Black men I knew had to stay in the back, cook, and keep their heads down—they weren't allowed to own businesses.

Yet what Mama and I saw that day at our lunch was a way to bring customers back and make them proud of our heritage. Barbeque was the answer to our prayers. It kept our family afloat, both financially and spiritually. I will never forget that moment when everything changed for our family. It felt like my grandfather and father were my guardian angels.

For me, barbeque has always been synonymous with celebrations. When I was a kid in the 1950s, we barbequed to celebrate family achievements and things like the end of the tobacco harvest season. It was the only time during my childhood when Blacks and whites ate side by side. For a brief moment, we were colorblind,

and I never forgot that feeling. The next time I experienced it was in Vietnam, when guys around me were being wounded and killed. The only way we were going to get home alive, besides our prayers, was by watching one another's backs. I've realized that when we have a common need to exist, everything else goes out the window: color, ethnicity, religion, gender, anything that can be divisive.

Barbeque still has that power today.

Drive an hour southeast from Wilson to Pete Jones's Skylight Inn BBQ in Ayden, North Carolina, and inside you'll see whites and Blacks eating whole-hog barbeque together. In my generation, that particular part of North Carolina was rife with racial tension, and for our safety, we stayed away as much as possible. Today, you see Black, whites, and every color eating barbeque together. Every time I go down there, I think of that.

And yet for many, barbeque is a topic as controversial as race or religion. Together, these make up three pillars of our Southern identity that are intricately linked—each person fervently believing that his or hers is the best. Each region stakes claim to its own barbeque style based on animal type, cut of meat, charcoal, wood, and sauce.

I've tried, as many pitmasters do, to embrace these differences and focus on

the beauty of what barbeque means—peace and good eating. As a result, I've often overlooked the fact that to me, barbeque is African American food. My enslaved ancestors stood over their enslavers' pits. They were always connected to the land, by force and by ancestral wisdom they carried over on ships. They grew collards in their small gardens, and those collards provided the vitamins for them to survive through the worst of times. Plantation owners handed offal—chitlins, pickled pigs' feet, snouts, and ears—to the field hands. And the enslaved cooked them to perfection, until they became delicacies. My matriarchal ancestors were plantation chefs, the skilled cooks who created the soul food that fed the American South from the mid-1600s until well after the antebellum period.

So why, then, are only a handful of African American entrepreneurs barbequing whole hog today? Rodney Scott in Hemingway, South Carolina; Dr. Howard Conyers in Manning, South Carolina; and Bryan Furman in Atlanta, Georgia are some of the great ones. But look around. Most of the pitmasters on the barbeque circuit are white. There are countless books on barbeque, but show me an African American author telling the story of his or her ancestors and their food. Is it because African Americans consider this type of work too reminiscent of the servitude of their ancestors, or is it because starting a barbeque restaurant today takes hundreds of thousands of dollars? Systemic racism permeates the food and agriculture business, so resources and interest play a part. I reckon it's a bit of both.

As far back as I can remember, and even still today, Black-owned restaurants in Wilson would sneak a barbeque sandwich on the menu and serve it as a side. We just knew that they had the power to make sure that we never owned a full-scale barbeque restaurant even though we were doing all the cooking at every plantation barbeque and political rally, and in their kitchens. After Daddy died in 1991 and I decided barbeque was my career and legacy, I got in it to win it. When we designed our menu, we were intentional about adding dishes that we served in our home. Traditional dishes that so many Black families in Wilson ate at home or at a pig pickin', a traditional North Carolina barbeque. Daily, we served collard greens with backbones, ribs, pigs' feet, cracklin', and so much more. My son, Ryan, got involved out of necessity. Now that Mitchell's BBQ was a full-time job, we needed all hands on deck. I insisted that he learn the craft and earn those Air Jordans his generation loved to wear.

I barbeque not because I love hoisting 150-pound hogs over my shoulders, but because I want to keep the tradition of my African American ancestors alive. My decision to team up with my son was strategic. The minute he showed interest in my work, I wanted him involved, because barbeque has always been a family affair to me. I wanted him to come home after he experienced working for corporate America. I needed Ryan's help to move this family business forward.

When he was in college, Ryan told me, "I want to own five or six restaurants." I encouraged him to pursue a degree in business and economics so he could help me run the restaurant, reminding him that the family business was his legacy. I was so glad that he came on board to help me out. I know a lot of fathers whose children aren't interested in the family business. God truly blessed me. It was challenging for me without his help. I was tired. The management side, on top of cooking every day, was a lot to manage.

Today, I barbeque to show young African Americans that our history lies in those embers. I wear overalls and a baseball cap, like those worn by my grandfather Lawyer Sandars and other Black men from previous generations, to remind me of the sacrifices of the men

who wore this uniform, who worked the land and provided for their families. It makes me realize that the work I do, while it can seem futile at times, is important. After all, I am one of the last barbeque pitmasters who knows how to cook a whole hog like my ancestors did.

Building a Fire

Mastering the craft of barbeque takes practice and motivation. It requires a sincere commitment to learning a skill set called *banking the coals*, something I learned from Mr. James Kirby, an elder and family friend in Wilson. I was taught the opposite of what most people are taught.

Most people are taught to cook whole-hog barbeque low and slow. My way is to start the coals at a high temperature and taper them down. The high heat breaks down all the muscles and cartilage in the meat, making it so succulent. These are essential steps to the Ed Mitchell method of banking the coals.

1. Prepare your grill.
2. Let the coals reach a high temperature, 400° to 500°F.
3. Turn off the draft (this is the banking process).
4. Allow the coals to sit and simmer, creating pure heat for 20 minutes. They won't flare up.
5. Square off the coals, aligning them on the inside of the grill.
6. Place a large number of coals on the shoulders and the left and right ham.
7. Leave the middle of the grill empty, making a square around the hog so that all the larger cuts of meat cook in unison.

Prepping the grill and the coals is essential to cooking a perfect piece of meat.

Choose a 115- to 120-pound whole hog, the ideal size for whole-hog barbeque. Larger hogs require more coals and more attention.

1

WHOLE-HOG BARBEQUE, PITS, AND FIRE

Pitboys to Pitmasters

It was important to my family and me that we cook the old-fashioned way. The way my grandfather, my father, and Mr. Kirby taught me. I wanted to celebrate the skill sets of both the pitmaster and the matriarchs in my family and community, who made all the side dishes to complement the whole-hog barbeque we made every day at Mitchell's Ribs, Chicken & Bar-B-Q. Our customers knew they were going to get farm-raised chicken, barbeque, and side dishes prepared the way our grandparents had cooked. This set us apart from the other restaurants in Wilson. We were living a farm-to-table lifestyle before it became en vogue. We all grew up eating farm-raised food, from hogs to greens. It's all we knew.

Night befo' dem barbeques, I used to stay up all night a-cooking and basting de meats wid barbeque sass (sauce). It made of vinegar, black and red pepper, salt, butter, a little sage, coriander, basil, onion, and garlic. Some folks drop a little sugar in it.

On a long pronged stick I wraps a soft rag or cotton fer a swab, and all de night long I swabe dat meat 'till it drip into de fire. Dem drippings change de smoke into seasoned fumes dat smoke de meat. We turn de meat over and swab it dat way all night long 'till it ooze seasoning and bake all through.

—Wesley Jones, Slave Narratives (Volume XIV, June 21, 1937)*

In the old days, on the plantation, slave owners would call us *pitboys* when they wanted to have a barbeque. Today, we are *pitmasters*. When it came time to barbeque on those plantations, they always called for the oldest enslaved male on the plantation. The white planters knew the pitboy had mastered the barbeque skill set, and they wanted that hog to be cooked to perfection. During the hog killing, the white planters would give what they considered the undesirable parts of the hog to the old pitboy. (We weren't allowed to eat high on the hog. The big house dined on all the entrées we made.) That old pitboy would take the inner parts of the hog, the offal, to the cabins, where up to twelve people were living inside. The matriarch or grandmother had to figure out what to do with what they had available to feed all of us. In the old days, food was about survival and finding some type of joy and celebration in what we cooked after a long day in the fields or cooking for the big house.

They mastered the craft of cooking whole-hog barbeque and accompanying side dishes, both the men and women. You can't just go out there and get some charcoal and fire and think that you are going to make a perfectly cooked whole hog. Whole-hog barbeque is a labor of love, an art. It is legacy, passed down from family to family. If I can help preserve the art of whole-hog barbeque and teach the craft to aspiring young chefs, they will be unstoppable.

* *This and the other narratives collected by the Federal Writers' Project are important records, but these oral histories were recorded in the 1930s by white writers and the language reflects this. The ingredients used and methods of cooking barbeque in these narratives were echoed in early documents of African American barbeque pitmasters.*

PITBOY, *barbeque artist*, and *pitmaster* were terms used to describe African American barbeque men and some women in the nineteenth through twenty-first centuries. Eastern North Carolina's most prominent African American "barbeque artist," Reverend Adam W. Scott of Goldsboro, North Carolina, was crowned as "N.C. Barbecue King" in a September 3, 1938, article. In numerous articles from the 1930s to the '60s, Reverend Scott, a former bank messenger and whole-hog barbeque caterer, was lauded for cooking forty to sixty hogs at a time for the "richest families of the city" and shipping barbeque to Mexico, Bermuda, "homesick Tarheels," and two of his best customers in Hollywood, Bob Hope and Ava Gardner. Reverend Scott said that his barbeque sauce was "divinely revealed to him in a dream." Scott's barbeque sauce and the Scott family's four barbeque houses in Goldsboro earned them accolades and created a family fortune and a rich legacy for Eastern North Carolina barbeque history.

The Mitchells' Eastern North Carolina Old-Fashioned Whole-Hog Barbeque

Serves 75 • **Prep Time:** 1 hour • **Cooking Time:** 7 hours

When I first went to the bank in 1997 with my idea of expanding the grocery store into a restaurant and including a barbeque university, their answer was an immediate no. My dream was to open Mitchell's Ribs, Bar-B-Q & Chicken in East Wilson, a predominately African American neighborhood where our only businesses were beauty supply stores, liquor stores, and a few mom-and-pop restaurants. Our dollars, communities, and brilliance are always seen as risky investments by banks, even while our labor during slavery was the backbone of so many industries, creating incalculable wealth. We just want an equitable and non-prejudicial opportunity to raise the capital we need to launch or expand our businesses and raise our families. Thank God I was able to find a reputable and respected African American businessman from Wilson to invest. That investor, Erader Mills, believed in my vision and wanted to see something other than a liquor store on the east side of Wilson.

I wasn't thinking about fame, fortune, or politics. I just wanted to make my family, my son, those who came before me, and my community proud. I just wanted to cook as I was taught, using the best products. I always use the analogy of gasoline: When you pull up to the pump at the gas station, you have a choice: regular, midgrade, or premium. For me as a pitmaster, premium is always the best choice, and that means free-range hogs raised on small farms; they taste better and remind me of my childhood in Wilson. There is no comparison. In the nineties, it was controversial for me to say that. Maybe it still is.

I WILL NEVER FORGET WHEN I was cooking at a festival and some white commercial hog farmers came up to me, threatening me and telling me I needed to stop advocating for hogs that are fed non-GMO diets. I didn't realize that my voice had power and would cause such an uproar. I just wanted to cook how I was taught and feed my customers what I would eat. I said to myself, *Damn, all I want to do is cook a little barbeque and keep the flavor from when I grew up.* I didn't realize I was about to get into a political whirlwind and legal battle. My mission has always been focused on the craft of barbeque, not on the politics of the pork industry.

This recipe is a rendition of our generational old-fashioned whole-hog barbeque.

1 gallon apple cider vinegar

½ cup of salt and ¼ ground black pepper

5 teaspoons smoked paprika

5 teaspoons ground sage

½ cup red pepper flakes

1 (100-pound) pasteurized whole hog

FIRST, bank your coals on your grill (see page 9). Mix the vinegar, salt, black pepper, paprika, sage, and red pepper flakes in a jug and set aside the vinegar-based sauce. Prepare the charcoal inside the smoker at the bottom of the barrel. Once the charcoals are white hot, square them off on the grill. Put your top grate on top of the smoker. Lay the hog skin-side up on the grate. Ensure there is an even amount of charcoal on the hams and shoulders on each side. This process creates a homemade convection oven. The key to not have the grease flame up is positioning the coals around the hog. You eliminate any flare-ups by not placing the coals in the middle. Close the lid and open your side draft vents and let it simmer at 300° to 350°F. You have to trust the process and let the hog cook for 7 hours, making sure there are no weather variations with wind or rain. Use a thermometer gauge placed on top of the closed grill. After 7 hours, stick your thermometer in the hog's back leg; if the thermometer is reading 180°F, then the hog is cooked.

FLIP the hog, then begin to debone the animal, remove gristle and discards, and begin chopping the meat with a cleaver as you go. Use a barbeque sauce basting mop to evenly distribute about a cup of the vinegar barbeque sauce on the cooked hog.

Red Clay Pork Cracklin'

Serves 15 • **Prep Time:** 30 minutes • **Cooking Time:** 15 minutes

North Carolina is one of the most beautiful states in the South. The lush green pine trees along with the coastal and mountainous regions with rivers that run through our great state provide us with everything we need, if we take care of them. The red clay soil in the Piedmont region reminds me of our cracklin': hints of the golden sun and the soil so rich and red it provides all the nutrients, joy, and abundance we all deserve.

Black folks and the Indigenous peoples of North Carolina were the guardians of this land. Maybe that's why I advocate so much for small farmers, because we have always been the ones growing the food, even through our pain; the land was our connection to each generation.

> WE ATE TO SURVIVE. WHAT WE THOUGHT WAS EVERYDAY COOKING, OTHERS WILL THINK YOU HUNG THE MOON WHEN THEY TASTE IT.
>
> —Ed Mitchell

When John T. Edge invited us to participate in the 2002 Southern Foodways Alliance Symposium in Oxford, Mississippi, we made fresh cracklin' for the attendees. They had heard of cracklin' before but never tried it as a main ingredient added to whole-hog barbeque. All the major food writers were there. When I demonstrated how to make crunchy crispy golden cracklin' and showed them how we add it to cooked whole-hog barbeque, you would have thought that I hung the moon, the way they looked at me with awe. It was so simple to us, and we served it that way all the time back home in Wilson. We served cracklin' barbeque sandwiches at our restaurant—thin-layered crispy golden pork skin mixed with our shredded whole hog and served between slices of white bread with our Eastern North Carolina vinegar BBQ sauce was a favorite.

People would come to our restaurant just to buy bags of the skin. For the Big Apple Barbecue Block Party in New York, we walked around with fresh cracklin' in a pan as samples, and festival attendees went nuts for it.

Cooked whole-hog skin

HULL out the inside of the hog after flipping the hog and deboning and removing the cooked meat. The skin will come off easily. Lay the cooked pork cracklin' on the grill and cook at a medium temperature until the skin is parched and crispy golden brown on both sides.

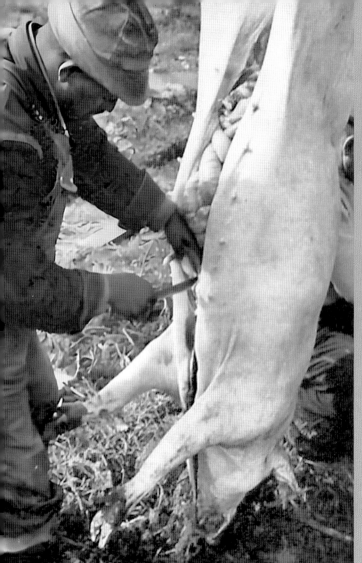

HOG SLAUGHTER
IN 1941

NEWS BUREAU PHOTO NO. 4188

NORTH CAROLINA DEPARTMENT OF
CONSERVATION AND DEVELOPMENT

This common ritual of slaughtering hogs
was a collaboration of neighbors, families,
churches, and farmers and lasted well into
the twentieth century.

Hog killing was a communal event that relied on the entire community to pitch in to salt, smoke, butcher, barbeque, and preserve all parts of the hog for yearly living. Landowners, sharecroppers, tenant farmers, and families used every part of the hog to make lard, lye soap, sausages, chitterlings, souse meat, pickled pork, ham, bacon, and other by-products.

Fresh Farm Lard

Serves 5 • **Prep Time:** 10 minutes • **Cooking Time:** 10 minutes

In the South, especially in the Carolinas, hog killing is the best time to make lard. If you are of a certain generation or grew up in the South, every grandmother had a lard can on her stove. The flavor is in the lard; bacon and hog renderings flavor greens, fried chicken, stews, beans, pie crusts, and biscuits. Nothing is wasted.

In my youth, everyone participated in hog-killing day. When I was growing up, we knew exactly where our food came from and what was in it. On hog-killing day, every part of the hog was salted, preserved, smoked, scrambled, or barbequed. Hog-killing day was a day we feasted. The older generation knew how to stretch food and use every part of the animal to survive, making soap, sausage, salted smoked ham, fatback, bacon, lard, and so on. God bless them.

Fatty hog meat, quartered, or thick-cut bacon

IN a large, deep cast-iron skillet, cook the hog meat or bacon over medium heat. Add ⅓ cup water so that the meat won't stick. Cook for 45 minutes, or until the meat renders about 1 cup of grease, adding water when needed. Remove the pan from the heat, remove the meat, and allow the lard to congeal. Transfer the lard to a mason jar with a spoon. You can use a fine sieve or colander to remove any meat bits. Cover and store at room temperature.

2

APPETIZERS

My Granddaddy Lawyer Sandars's Farm, and My Parents' Story

LAWYER SANDARS, May 9, 1888–January 30, 1959

My grandfather Lawyer Sandars, my mother Doretha's father, was born on a farm in Wilson, North Carolina, in 1888. Granddaddy Lawyer was a sharecropper and wore large denim bib overalls. Every day, I wear overalls to honor him. He always carried two wallets. Back in those days, there were no banks that would help us, but Granddaddy would always loan money to those in need. He was his own mutual aid society, and was well respected in the community. "You can't spend it twice," he would say to teach me about spending and saving. As his grandchild, if you did something special, he would reward you. He taught me so many lessons about life, work, and family.

Granddaddy was a stout, robust man, always jolly and bubbly. He grew peanuts and sweet potatoes. I remember all the large barrels of molasses and flour at his farm. We always had something to eat, and he loved to eat food right from the farm!

Granddaddy liked my dad, Willie, but my grandmother Beatrice Sandars didn't care for my father initially because he was fair-skinned. She was afraid that he would think he was better than them because they were dark-skinned. Nevertheless, my father was determined to win my mother's hand in marriage. Back then, you had to have permission from the entire family, especially the father.

My father, William "Willie" Mitchell, was my hero. He was a hardworking man, and I think my grandfather saw a light in him. Granddaddy eventually took him under his wing and taught my father the art of barbeque. He lived by the mantra "Your word is your bond." What he said was the law of the land. If he said something, you could depend on him to deliver. He raised my brothers and me to be like him. I respected him so much.

My dad had a troubled childhood. He was born out of wedlock, and when his mother married, he took the last name of his stepfather: Mitchell. His stepfather was abusive; he would kick my father out and my dad would crawl under the house,

hiding underneath the wood floors, where he could see into the cracks of the kitchen floor. His mother would come and console my father after he'd been arguing with his stepfather. It was sad hearing how hard his childhood was. I'm sure he wanted to make sure he treated my mother and his children better.

Daddy fell in love with my mother after meeting her through her brother, his best friend. They had a seven-year age gap between them at a time when women married very young and had children young. My mother was ready to leave her birth home. Her father had a built-in workforce—he had ten children from a previous marriage, plus twenty-five children with my grandmother, and my mama needed a break. She was tired of sharing whatever she earned from selling huckleberries on the side of the road with her siblings. Every time she bought something for herself, she had no choice but to share. Mama said, "I grew up with so many siblings, I knew I wanted a smaller family."

When my parents married in the 1940s, my dad moved my mother into town in Wilson. He didn't want her living on the farm with him. Sharecropping, working in the tobacco fields from sunup to sundown, was a hard life. Later, my dad started working at the ABC store, a liquor store run by North Carolina's alcoholic

Doretha, had an eighth-grade education, they were the smartest, most business-savvy, and most God-fearing couple I knew. My mother was so smart one of her teachers wanted to adopt her to make sure she pursued an education, but her parents wouldn't agree. Granddaddy would say, "This the smartest gal I got, doggone it."

AUBREY MITCHELL, middle son of Willie and Doretha Mitchell

They raised us the right way. Daddy was a good father and provider. He would give you his left arm and didn't mind helping people. He spent time with us and taught us how to be men and carry ourselves. How to treat women and how to barbeque. He was good with numbers. He would say, "A chicken can lay six eggs, but that doesn't mean you will have six chicks. You have to wait until they hatch to count your chickens." I learned a lot also from my big brother, Ed, and my mother. We come from good stock.

STEVIE MITCHELL, youngest son of Willie and Doretha Mitchell

Daddy didn't waver. He was a pillar in the community. He threw down when he cooked barbeque, and Mama showed us how to cook with the oven. She is ninety-one years old, and she's still full of energy and cooking exactly how she cooked when we were children.

beverage commission, where he stocked shelves, and Mama worked as a domestic cook in the homes of tobacco factory managers and on many of the plantations in North Carolina. My dad worked at the ABC store for thirty-five years until he retired at sixty-five. Mama worked for the affluent Herring family for fifteen years, cleaning and cooking. They bought the store with their life savings. It was their pride and joy. They would spend all day there, even cook their meals there, and their customers were our neighbors and friends.

Although my father, Willie, only had a third-grade education and my mother,

ON MAY 2, 1940, the *Wilson Daily Times* interviewed Ed Mitchell's grandfather Lawyer Sandars to confirm reports from a census taker that Sandars had fathered thirty-five children between his first and second wives. "Lawyer and his wife and ten of their 20 living children live in one room of a shack back on Wilson's Daniel Hill, negro section of the town. Lawyer—and that's his real name too—works on WPA in the daytime. He makes around $21 every two weeks for his large family and is happy." The article goes on to state that Sandars previously worked as a sharecropper for the majority of his life before working for the government. Beatrice Sandars, Lawyer's wife and Ed Mitchell's grandmother, called herself a "granny woman," noting that neither she nor her children ever went to the hospital or became ill. During slavery, it was common for enslavers to force enslaved persons to produce children, which for the enslaver meant more laborers. Enslaved persons were their main cash crop. As the sharecropping and tenant-farming system developed post–Civil War, prior physical bondage evolved into debt bondage. Early childbearing for both impoverished Black and white farm laborer families in the South was a form of economic survival, especially for non-landowners; children were once again commodified as assets, forever in debt to the landowner. According to Leon Dash in his *Washington Post* article "Children of the Old South," "Tobacco and cotton required months of bending, kneeling and careful picking, work that children did best . . . During the hard times and the good times, the survival or prosperity of the tenant farmer was tied directly to the labor of his children . . . the more children a tenant-farming family had, the larger the landlord's profit." Lawyer Sandars's first wife, Dora Clark Sandars, left Wilson for the North after losing their last baby during childbirth. Dora never returned to Wilson and was assumed to have died.

Cracklin' Hush Puppies

Serves 5 • **Prep Time:** 10 minutes • **Cook Time**: 20 minutes

In 1993, Tony, one of our chefs, was freestyling in the kitchen and making some food for himself on his break. He took some cracklin' crumbs, added them to our hush puppy batter, and fried them. As soon as Ryan tried Tony's cracklin' hush puppies, they became a household favorite.

Canola oil, for frying

1 cup self-rising cornmeal

½ cup self-rising flour

2 tablespoons finely chopped onion

1 medium-sized egg, beaten

¾ cup buttermilk

2 tablespoons honey

½ cup crumbled fresh crispy pork cracklin'

True Made Foods' Carolina Gold BBQ Sauce or tartar sauce, for serving

HEAT oil in a deep fryer or high-sided frying pan to 350°F (if using a frying pan, make sure you use enough oil for the hush puppies to float). In a large bowl, stir together the cornmeal, flour, and onion. Stir in the egg, buttermilk, and honey. Let the mixture sit for 10 minutes, then stir again, but this time add the pork cracklin'. It's important to add the cracklin' last to hold its crisp texture. Working in batches, drop the batter by the tablespoon into the hot oil (or portion it into the oil with a small ice cream scoop). Fry until the hush puppies are golden brown or start to float. Drain on a paper towel and enjoy them nice and hot. Serve with BBQ sauce or tartar sauce.

Let 'Em Roll Fried Green Tomatoes

Serves 4 • **Prep Time:** 10 minutes • **Cook Time:** 10 minutes

Fried green tomatoes were a side dish my mother made to go along with our barbeque. We started visiting other barbeque restaurants in other cities and saw fried green tomatoes on their menus, so we added Mama's fried green tomatoes to our menu. They became a hit in both North Carolina and New York. Season your tomatoes, batter them in flour, put them in your oil, and let 'em roll.

4 green tomatoes

Salt and freshly ground black pepper

1 cup all-purpose flour

1 teaspoon garlic powder

Dash of sugar

2 eggs

2 cups bread crumbs

1 teaspoon onion powder

1 teaspoon Italian seasoning

Vegetable or canola oil, for frying

Pimento cheese and cooked bacon or fried pork belly, for serving

CUT each green tomato into ½-inch-thick slices. Pat with a paper towel to remove some of the moisture. Season with salt and pepper to taste.

IN a shallow dish, combine the flour, garlic powder and sugar, plus salt and pepper to taste. Whisk the eggs in a medium bowl. In another shallow dish, combine the bread crumbs, onion powder, and Italian seasoning.

COAT each green tomato slice in the flour mixture, then dip it into the egg mixture, and finally dredge it in the bread crumb mixture, making sure that each slice is fully dressed. Fry 3 or 4 slices at a time for 3 to 4 minutes on each side, until golden brown in a fryer or in a deep pan on low-medium heat. Drain them on paper towels. Top with pimento cheese and cooked bacon or fried pork belly.

Creamy Deviled Eggs

Serves 6 • **Prep Time:** 20 minutes • **Cook Time:** 15 minutes

Creamy deviled eggs are Ryan's personal favorite dish that Mama would make every Thanksgiving. She made several dozen because she knew he would happily eat a dozen by himself.

6 large eggs

1 cup Miracle Whip

¼ cup sweet salad relish

1 tablespoon yellow mustard

½ teaspoon chopped fresh dill

Salt and freshly ground black pepper

½ teaspoon paprika

PUT the eggs in a medium pot and cover with water. Bring to a boil over high heat. Lower the heat to medium-high and boil for about 15 minutes. Here is a tip: When you see one of the eggs crack in the pot, you know they're done. Run the eggs under room-temperature water to cool them and peel.

HALVE the eggs vertically and scoop out the yolks with a regular spoon, placing them in a medium bowl. Using the back of a fork, mash the yolks in the bowl. Add the Miracle Whip, relish, mustard, dill, and a dash each of salt and pepper, then mix until combined.

PIPE the egg yolk mixture into each egg white half. Sprinkle each deviled egg lightly with paprika. Cover the deviled eggs and chill in the refrigerator for 15 minutes before serving.

Smoked Collard Green Dip

Serves 5 • **Prep Time:** 10 minutes • **Cook Time:** 25 minutes

In 2016, the *Today* show invited us up to represent the Carolina Panthers at their BBQ Super Bowl showdown. In an effort to move collard greens beyond their place as a side dish, my son, Ryan, developed this Southern take on the ever-popular spinach dip. We served this smoky-sweet dip in a sourdough bowl and won the game. Sadly, the Panthers did not win.

2 tablespoons extra-virgin olive oil

1 smoked ham hock, bone removed and discarded, meat chopped into ½-inch dice

½ large sweet onion, finely chopped

2 garlic cloves, minced

¼ cup dry white wine

1 (2-pound) bunch fresh collard greens, rinsed and cut into ¼-inch-wide, 1-inch-long slices, remove stems

1½ cups (8 ounces) cream cheese, cut into pieces

1 cup (8 ounces) sour cream

¾ cup freshly grated Parmesan cheese

½ teaspoon red pepper flakes, plus more if needed

Kosher salt and freshly ground black pepper

Butter, for greasing

Toast points, pita bread, tortilla chips, or silver dollar corn cakes (see page 87), for serving

IN a Dutch oven, heat the olive oil over medium heat. Once it's hot, add the ham, cover, and cook over medium-low heat for about 1 hour until the ham hock is golden brown. Transfer the ham to a paper towel–lined plate. Remove all but 2 tablespoons of the drippings from the Dutch oven. Set the Dutch oven back over medium heat. Add the onion and cook, stirring, until tender, about 5 minutes, then add the garlic and cook, stirring, for 30 seconds. Pour in the wine and simmer, stirring to loosen any particles from the bottom of the pan, for 1 to 2 minutes. Add the collard greens, cover the pan, and cook, stirring once or twice, until wilted, about 10 minutes. Add the cream cheese, sour cream, ½ cup of the Parmesan cheese, and the red pepper flakes. Season

liberally with salt and black pepper. Stir until the cream cheese has melted
and mixture is heated through, about 7 minutes. Taste, adding more salt,
black pepper, or red pepper flakes, if you choose. Transfer to a lightly buttered
1½-quart baking dish.

JUST before serving, set a rack in 6 inches from the broiler heating element
and set the oven to broil. Sprinkle the collard dip evenly with the remaining
¼ cup Parmesan. Broil until the cheese has lightly browned, 4 to 5 minutes.
Top with the diced ham and serve with toast points, pita bread, tortilla chips,
or corn cakes.

North Carolina Souse Meat (Hog's Head Cheese)

Serves 6 • **Prep Time:** 20 minutes, plus chilling overnight • **Cook Time:** 4½ hours

We call it "souse meat" in North Carolina. Souse meat is our version of hog's head cheese, a pork mixture seasoned to perfection with herbs and spices. We serve it cold like a pâté, with saltine crackers and Ed's Cayenne Hot Sauce. Mama makes souse meat from scratch. It is a delicacy for us. We served Anthony Bourdain souse meat when he filmed us for his show *A Cook's Tour* and he loved it.

3 pounds pig ears

1 pound hog maws

2 pounds pork neck bones

2 fresh cayenne peppers or your favorite hot peppers, diced (optional)

1 green bell pepper, diced

1 yellow onion, diced

¼ cup minced garlic

¼ cup kosher salt

2 tablespoons freshly ground black pepper

¼ cup dried oregano

¼ cup pickling spice

1 tablespoon ground allspice

2 tablespoons red pepper flakes

1½ cups apple cider vinegar

3 cups chicken broth

Vegetable oil

Ed's Cayenne Hot Sauce, for serving

Saltine crackers or bread, for serving

WASH all your meat thoroughly. Boil the pig ears in a medium stockpot filled with water for 30 minutes, or until tender. Drain the pig ears and set aside. Chop the hog maws into ¼-inch chunks, then separate the meat from the pork neck bones and chop into ¼-inch chunks. Set aside.

IN a large stockpot, combine the hog maws, pig ears, neck meat, cayenne pepper, bell pepper, onion, garlic, salt, black pepper, oregano, pickling spice, allspice, red pepper flakes, vinegar, and broth. Add water to cover the contents of the pot, if needed. Bring to a boil over medium-high heat, then lower the heat to medium-low and cook for 3 to 4 hours. Drain any remaining liquid and

cool the meat mixture for 10 minutes. Chop the meat. Remove and discard any remaining bones or cartilage.

OIL one standard loaf pan and add the meat mixture. Let the souse meat congeal. Add a cup of the neck bone liquid to the loaf pan. Cover the loaf pan with plastic wrap and refrigerate overnight. Cut the souse meat into ¼-inch-thick slices and serve with hot sauce and saltine crackers or bread.

Okra Poppers

Serves 4 • **Prep Time:** 8 minutes • **Cook Time:** 8 minutes

I love okra—fried, grilled, and in stews. We ate okra a lot back in the old days when my grandparents were alive. The old folks ate okra in all kinds of ways. They weren't scared of the slime—they loved it. Times change, and the newer generations prefer fried okra or okra prepared with minimal slime.

1 pound fresh okra pods

2 eggs

1½ teaspoons kosher salt, plus more if needed

Vegetable oil, for frying

1¼ cups yellow cornmeal

¼ cup all-purpose flour

½ teaspoon freshly ground black pepper

¼ teaspoon cayenne pepper

¼ teaspoon paprika

True Made Foods Honey Mustard, for serving

CUT the okra crosswise into ½-inch-wide pieces, discarding the tips. In a medium bowl, lightly beat the eggs with ½ teaspoon of the salt. Add the okra and fully coat with the egg mixture. Let the okra soak for 10 minutes.

HEAT oil in a large cast-iron skillet or deep fryer to 350°F.

IN a double-layered medium brown paper bag, mix the cornmeal, flour, remaining 1 teaspoon salt, the black pepper, cayenne, and paprika. Add the okra to the cornmeal mixture, shake, and toss to coat.

WHEN the oil is ready, remove the okra from the cornmeal mixture with a slotted spoon and fry until light golden brown, 2 to 3 minutes. Remove the okra from the oil with a slotted spoon, allowing any excess oil to drain off, then transfer to a paper towel–lined plate. Finish with a sprinkle of salt, if desired. We serve this with honey mustard for a delicious dipping delight.

Ryan's Cracklin'-Crusted Chicken Wings

Serves 3 to 5 • **Prep Time:** 10 minutes • **Cook Time:** 8 minutes

RYAN MITCHELL, Ed Mitchell's son

I knew that my generation loved wings and tailgating for games like Duke University vs. UNC. The trick to our wings is smoking them first and then dipping them in our Pork Panko crumbs and flash-frying them before serving.

15 to 20 chicken wings (medium-sized recommended)

2 tablespoons True Made Foods Ed's "Mother of All" Spice Rub, plus more for seasoning the wings

Oak wood chips

Canola oil

1 medium-sized egg

½ cup buttermilk

1 cup fresh cracklin' crumbs (pulsed in food processor) or Pork Panko

SEASON the wings with Ed's "Mother of All" spice rub.

USING oak wood chips, establish a 250°F fire in your smoker. Place the wings on an oiled grate and set it about 12 inches above the coals. Close the smoker and wait 30 minutes before flipping. After the first hour, start flipping every 20 minutes and moving the wings to finish evenly. Cooking time will vary from 1½ to 2 hours. Let cool for 15 to 20 minutes.

MIX the egg and buttermilk in a medium bowl. In another bowl, mix the cracklin' crumbs and the 2 tablespoons "Mother of All" spice rub. Add the smoked wings to the egg mixture, shake, then dip in the panko. Cover the wings in the egg mixture again and shake off any excess. Refrigerate the coated wings for 30 minutes or more to set the crust.

HEAT oil in a deep fryer to 350°F. Flash-fry the wings for 2 to 3 minutes, until golden brown.

Rib Tips with Ed's Memphis Barbeque Sauce

Serves 8 • **Prep Time:** 10 minutes • **Cook Time:** 4 hours

We didn't know that Chicago had a rib tip history and culture. We were just trying to find a way to cut our overhead costs and not waste product. Waste not, want not! That's the pitmaster's secret principle when it comes to rib tips.

I wanted to add a finger food appetizer to the menu. When I introduced the idea to serve rib tips, our partners and cooks said, "Who is going to eat gristle?" Well, our customers loved it, and clearly I was thinking like Black pitmasters from Chicago did almost a hundred years ago when they left the South and had to make a way out of no way.

To cut rib tips, you have to take a full slab of unprocessed spareribs, or untrimmed spareribs. The trimmed parts that you would normally discard are the BEST part.

½ cup True Made Foods Ed's Undefeated Legend Rib Rub

½ cup of True Made Foods Ed's Kansas City BBQ Sauce

5 pounds pork rib tips

MIX the rib rub and BBQ sauce in a medium bowl. Generously spread the mixture on the rib tips. Refrigerate for at least 2 hours or overnight.

SMOKE the rib tips at between 225° and 250°F for 3 to 4 hours. First, get your coals hot. The coal temperature should reach 350°F. Use the indirect cooking method, where the coals are placed on one side of the smoker and the other side is bare. Place the rib tips over the hot side of the grill for the first 10 minutes of cooking. Then offset the rib tips indirectly away from heat for the remainder of the cook time to slow smoke. If desired, for the last 30 minutes of cooking, baste the rib tips with more BBQ sauce, wrap in aluminum foil, and place them back on the grill over indirect heat for tenderness.

PULL the rib tips from the grill and allow to rest for 5 minutes. Chop the rib tips into smaller pieces before serving.

3

PORK AND BEEF

A Perfect Piece of Meat

All eyes were on me and my brothers, Aubrey and Stevie, at the Southern Foodways Alliance barbeque symposium in Oxford, Mississippi, in 2002. For every large festival or major event, we transport our smokers on an 18-wheeler. At the SFA barbeque symposium, there were pitmasters from all over the country who brought their fancy shiny lacquered grills and cooking gadgets. When our truck arrived, Aubrey and Stevie took the old smokers off the truck. A few of the fancy pitmasters laughed at us. We paid them no mind.

It started raining. Aubrey picked up our cooker and we sheltered under a willow tree. My brothers got the cooker good and hot and we went to work. We cooked a perfect whole hog with all the fixin's.

We had the last laugh.

BARBEQUE AT BRASWELL PLANTATION SEPTEMBER 1944

NEWS BUREAU
PHOTO NO. 4650 ½

NORTH CAROLINA DEPARTMENT OF
CONSERVATION AND DEVELOPMENT

The former Braswell Plantation near Rocky Mount, North Carolina, hosted annual summer farm dinners to celebrate a good harvest and award tenant farmers cash or food prizes. In November 1940, the *Southern Planter* published an article detailing the dinner that hosted 150 families. "Since early the night before, over 1,500 pounds of fine pig meat had been simmering over hot, hardwood coals. For hours Brunswick stew had been bubbling in iron wash pots. A special pot of pigs' feet and ears had been cooking and smelling as only a good Negro cook can make them smell." Whole hog barbecue was a treat during harvest season.

The *New York Times* and so many food writers wrote about me that day. They couldn't stop raving about our barbeque. We had that cracklin' crispy and golden mixed with a perfectly cooked pig. I couldn't have done it without my support system, our family and extended family. Participating in the SFA barbeque symposium made me realize that barbeque was bigger than Wilson, North Carolina.

After the barbeque symposium, Peter Kaminsky, a prestigious *New York Times* food writer, was researching the history of the Ossabaw Island hog, a free-range pig and direct descendant of the original hog breeds brought to the North America by the Spanish in the 1500s. In 2003, Peter arranged for me to cook the Ossabaw heritage breed. It was the most succulent and sweetest-tasting barbeque I had ever eaten, and it reminded me of the barbeque I ate as a boy. I had to figure out how to add old-fashioned pork like those Ossabaw pigs to my menu. So many thoughts ran through my head: Could I afford to purchase heritage breed hogs? Would my customers appreciate our menu change and buy the barbeque? What farmers were selling natural hogs in North Carolina?

John T. Edge and Peter suggested that I connect with North Carolina Agricultural and Technical State University, a historically Black college and university (HBCU) in Greensboro, North Carolina. A&T has always been a pillar in the Black community in North Carolina. Historically, they have always worked with Black farmers, and I have fond memories of the A&T students who were part of the civil rights movement sit-in at the Woolworth lunch counter in Greensboro in 1960. North Carolina A&T and I signed a Memorandum of Understanding with their College of Agriculture and Environmental Sciences. The university would research and develop reports on what hog breeds were the best for cooking barbeque, and I would provide the culinary expertise and become a brand ambassador. We just wanted to help Black farmers, who were destitute after the fall of tobacco, to provide a better product for my customers, and to hopefully encourage others to purchase from Black farmers. In 2004, we held a press conference to announce our partnership with North Carolina A&T University and our initiative with North Carolina Black farmers to bring natural hogs back into barbeque.

But the next thing I knew, my bank called and said that I had to pay $700,000 of my bank note immediately or they would foreclose on my business. I asked them to give me some time to pay.

I pleaded with them and told them that I would refinance and do whatever it took to keep our doors open.

I had previously contacted another bank to refinance my loan and presented my business plan, and they were very interested in refinancing my loan. A few of the bankers even came to my press conference. Food writers, television networks, and universities were all calling me to partner. I was just about to take off. Within twenty-nine days, my bank foreclosed my restaurant. My parents' supermarket, which I had turned into a restaurant, was taken from me. My employees and my family were now without jobs. I was heartbroken.

A week after the press conference, someone from the North Carolina Department of Revenue called me and said, "Mr. Mitchell, we are going to audit you. You are being investigated." I had nothing to hide, and their investigators came plenty of times to go through all my financial records. Many of them had eaten at my restaurant and knew me. They said, "Mr. Mitchell, we're going to charge you."

I said, "You're going to charge me?"

They said, "Yes, we're going to charge you."

I said, "Charge me with what?"

And they said, "We're going to charge you with embezzlement."

I was in shock. "Embezzlement? Embezzling what?"

"We're going to charge you with embezzling sales taxes."

I said, "You—you're joking, aren't you? You—you can't be serious."

With stoic faces, they said, "We're serious. We're going to give you three days to hire an attorney, and you will need to come to Raleigh for an arraignment." It felt like the floor underneath me had caved in.

Less than thirty days after my press conference, my restaurant had been foreclosed on and I was charged with embezzlement. My face was all over the news with headlines like "Ed Mitchell, BBQ Pitmaster, Charged with Embezzlement," suggesting that I was a thief. They officially charged me in Raleigh, put me on television, published articles, and tried to defame my character. But you know what? I'm a spiritual guy. I fell to my knees and prayed. Everyone in my family did, too, and I knew my mama's prayers would be heard.

When they charged me, I knew something wasn't right and that my day of vindication would come. My angel investor, Erader Mills, called me after the press fiasco and my arrest and helped me to hire a team of attorneys. His investment was also at stake. One thing I learned quickly is that Black entrepreneurs can never be late on payments. There is no room for a learning curve, and if we make a mistake, no matter how small, we rarely get just a slap on the wrist. Most businesses will be offered payment plans over an agreed-upon time period. You have to stay on top of the business of the restaurant even if you also have to man the pit and manage your employees. I take accountability for what I did and not paying on time, but it was too much of a coincidence.

In May 2007, Mr. Mills and I filed a racial discrimination suit against the bank. On January 19, 2008, the *Wilson Daily Times* announced our vindication: "Mills filed a countersuit to the bank's complaint, claiming the bank unlawfully foreclosed on the restaurant and unfairly handled loans." And we won! The Superior Court judge ruled that my bank improperly foreclosed on my restaurant. They found that the bank was in violation for not paying off the note owed to Mr. Mills before they could foreclose on me as an individual. If it wasn't for the support of Erader Mills, I surely would have lost everything my parents built, but most important, it was my mother's daily prayers that helped us through a rough storm.

I pled guilty to not paying my sales taxes on time. I spent thirty days in prison and was offered three years' probation. I also paid all that I owed to the state and then some. I still wonder, how many restaurant owners go to jail for being late on sales tax payments? I was sixty-one years old. Although we never reopened in Wilson, I was able to pay my investor back and keep the restaurant in our family.

AUBREY MITCHELL, middle son of Willie and Doretha Mitchell

Ed has always been before his time. My big brother had a real estate business in the 1980s with four secretaries. He was a pioneer in working with Black and small organic farmers. He worked with small farmers all over Eastern North Carolina, both Black and white. Many of the farmers have given up and moved on from raising hogs to growing vegetables due to the politics of pork and rising costs of feeding hogs.

Ed was always smart and a visionary. When you are before your time, people think you are strange. When they came after him, we knew they were wrong. They tried to break him. Ed stood his ground and didn't waver. He came back strong, and everyone loves a comeback story. We were always taught not to give up. He fought the system that tried to beat him, and in the end, he won.

NORTH CAROLINA has one of the largest commercial hog industries in America, ranking third in the nation. As of 2021, North Carolina had an estimated population of 10.5 million people, and on commercial hog farms in North Carolina, an estimated 9.5 million hogs are available for sale or consumption in an industry valued at $10 billion for the American consumer and for export to countries around the globe. Although the commercial hog industry has created thousands of jobs and opportunities for many, North Carolinians face tremendous challenges from the pollution associated with factory farming. Since the 1990s, the corporatization of the hog industry has come at a huge cost to the environment, and has created a political machine that has devoured many small hog farmers in North Carolina. North Carolina's most vulnerable residents, BIPOC, and working-class whites have fought for decades against environmental racism and classism. *The Smell of Money*, a 2022 documentary, examines the plight of rural Eastern North Carolina residents in a David-vs.-Goliath battle to bring attention to a huge public health and environmental crisis impacting the region's majority African American, Indigenous, and Latinx neighborhoods. In 2007, under the leadership of hog farmer Jeremiah Jones, a group of small free-range hog farmers organized to form the North Carolina Natural Hog Growers Association, a co-op of twenty-five certified non-GMO and third-party Animal Welfare Approved (AWA) hog farmers.

Mama Mitchell's Oven-Cooked Barbequed Shoulder

Serves 15 • **Prep Time:** 30 minutes • **Cooking Time:** 6 hours

During the holiday season and winter months, the smoker sat idle, but Mama's oven-cooked pork shoulder would always bring the backyard-barbeque feeling inside. Savory spices, red pepper vinegar sauce, and crispy cracklin' pieces were a taste of heaven. I'll never understand how one black pot could hold so much love!

1 tablespoon kosher salt

1 tablespoon light brown sugar

1 tablespoon paprika

1 tablespoon red pepper flakes

1 tablespoon ground cumin

1 tablespoon coarsely ground black pepper

1 tablespoon ground sage

1 (8- to 10-pound) skin-on pork shoulder

½ cup low-sodium chicken broth

½ cup apple cider vinegar

PREHEAT your oven to 350°F.

IN a medium bowl, combine the salt, brown sugar, paprika, red pepper flakes, cumin, black pepper, and sage. Set aside.

SET the pork shoulder skin-side up on your cutting board and gently score the skin in a crosshatch pattern with a sharp knife, making straight horizontal lines and then vertical ones. The meat should look like a checkerboard. Rub the spice mix into the cuts in the shoulder and on top of the skin until the meat is completely covered. Pour the broth into a deep roasting pan. Add the seasoned pork shoulder, skin-side up, cover with a piece of aluminum foil, and bake at 350°F for about 5 hours. Remove the foil and bake for 15 minutes more, or until the skin is light golden brown and a little crispy. During the 15-minute resting stage, ladle a ½ cup of apple cider vinegar over the barbequed shoulder.

Ed's Mouthwatering Baby Back Ribs

Serves 4 • **Prep Time:** 15 minutes • **Cooking Time:** 3 hours

These are the baby back ribs I used to defeat Bobby Flay on the Food Network television show *Throwdown with Bobby Flay*. Let me remind you that as a cook, I can't compete with Bobby Flay. The man is beyond talented. He just happened to challenge me on a dish I think I have mastered.

My rib technique involves smoking the racks for two hours, then steaming them with vinegar sauce for a few minutes, then drying them out again with more rub and smoke. The result is moist, fall-off-the-bone, winning ribs.

2 (12-rib) baby back rib racks

2 tablespoons Spanish paprika

2 tablespoons freshly ground black pepper

2 tablespoons dry mustard

2 tablespoons ground coriander

1 tablespoon ground cumin

2 tablespoons kosher salt

Olive oil

3 to 4 cups Ed's Eastern North Carolina Vinegar BBQ Sauce (page 74)

1 cup True Made Foods Ed's Kansas City Barbeque Sauce

THE night before cooking, rinse the ribs with water and pat dry with paper towels. Remove the skinlike membrane on the bone side of the ribs by sliding a paring knife underneath it. Grab the membrane, peel it off, and discard it.

COMBINE paprika, pepper, mustard, coriander, cumin, and salt in a small bowl. Rub both sides of the racks with just enough olive oil to coat them, then rub them on both sides with two-thirds of the spice mixture. (Reserve the remaining spice mixture for later.) Wrap the ribs in plastic wrap and refrigerate for at least 12 hours.

THE next day, prepare a grill for smoking the ribs. Preheat the grill to 225° to 250°F. Place the coals to one side of the grill. Once hot, place oak wood chunks on the hot, gray-white charcoal. Set the cooking grate over the fire, then place the ribs on the cooking grate on the opposite side from the coals so they cook

with indirect heat. Cover the grill, adjusting the vent to keep the temperature low, and smoke the ribs until a bone releases from the rack when tugged at, about 2 hours. (If the coals burn down, add more as needed.) Transfer the ribs to a large aluminum pan.

MIX the vinegar sauce and barbeque sauce in a bowl. Pour enough of the mixture into the pan to come ¼ inch up the sides; reserve the remaining mixture. Cover with plastic wrap and set back on the grill, but not directly above the coals. Cover the grill and let the ribs steam for about 15 minutes. Remove the ribs from the pan. Lightly dust them on both sides with the remaining spice mixture, then place them back on the grill, this time directly over the coals. Cover the grill and smoke until the ribs are dry on the outside but still moist inside, about 10 minutes. Serve with the remaining barbeque sauce mixture.

Lemon Pepper Bacon-Wrapped Pork Tenderloin

Serves 6 • **Prep Time:** 15 minutes • **Cooking Time:** 2 hours

Pork tenderloin was not a common dish in Eastern North Carolina. We added lemon pepper bacon-wrapped pork tenderloin to our menu after visiting New York. We were impressed by how New Yorkers served pork tenderloin as a haute menu item.

2 pounds pork tenderloin

1 teaspoon salt

1 teaspoon dried sage

1 teaspoon smoked paprika

½ teaspoon coarsely ground black pepper

8 to 10 slices thick-cut bacon

1 teaspoon lemon pepper seasoning

SET up your smoker for offset grilling and preheat to 275°F with a combination of charcoal and applewood chips. (Alternatively, preheat the oven to 325°F.)

PLACE the pork tenderloin on a baking sheet. Combine the salt, sage, smoked paprika, and black pepper in a small bowl and generously rub the spice mixture evenly all over the tenderloin. Wrap the bacon slices over the top of the pork tenderloin, folding the ends underneath the pork. Sprinkle the lemon pepper seasoning evenly over each piece of bacon.

SMOKE your pork tenderloin until the internal temperature reaches 170°F, or bake in the oven for 1 hour.

Rooter-to-Tooter Pork Chops

Serves 3 to 5 • **Prep Time:** 15 minutes • **Cooking Time:** 1 hour

My father, Willie, loved liver and onions, and my brothers and I loved pork chops. Most mothers would say, "You are going to eat what I serve." Our mother made what we liked. Cooking was her love language. Mama would say, "I cooked for years for rich folks, so I am going to make sure that my family eats well, too." My brothers, my son, and my nephews would come home from football practice and she would have a platter of chicken one day and then pork chops the next day. Everyone in our neighborhood knew they would get a plate of good food at Mother Mitchell's house. We were taught to cook every part of the hog, from the rooter to the tooter, and my mother's pork chops are still a favorite in our home.

4 cups water

¼ cup kosher salt

2 tablespoons date sugar

1 teaspoon whole black peppercorns

1 teaspoon smoked paprika

1 tablespoon red pepper flakes

5 (1¼-inch-thick) bone-in pork chops

2 tablespoons True Made Foods Ed's Carolina Classic Pork Rub

True Made Foods Ed's Carolina Red BBQ Sauce

IN a large cooking pot, bring the water almost to a boil over medium-low heat. Add the salt and date sugar. Whisk to dissolve. Whisk in the peppercorns, paprika, and red pepper flakes, then remove from heat and let cool for 30 minutes. Immerse the pork chops in the brine and refrigerate for 10 hours.

PREHEAT your smoker to 275°F (preferably with oak wood and charcoal). Prepare for indirect grilling for the first hour.

REMOVE pork chops from the brine and allow them to air-dry for 10 minutes. Season the pork chops on both sides with the rub. Place the pork chops in the smoker and cook over indirect heat until the temperature is at 130°F for about 1 hour. Then finish the pork chops directly over the coals until the temperature is 155°F. Transfer the chops to a large pan. Slather with BBQ sauce. Wrap the pan in aluminum foil and allow to rest for 10 minutes before serving.

Backyard Brisket

Serves 10 • **Prep Time:** 20 minutes • **Cooking Time:** 9 hours

You have to cook brisket slowly. I went to Michigan and cooked brisket for Andrew Zimmern, host of the Travel Channel show *Bizarre Foods with Andrew Zimmern*. I was surprised at how many people knew about me and my barbeque all the way in Michigan. When people invite you to cook in other cities, they remember you, especially if your food is good.

RYAN MITCHELL, Ed Mitchell's son

Brisket is the most scrutinized and sport-friendly piece of meat that is judged from every side. It has become commercialized. Not until we started traveling outside Wilson and met others on the barbeque circuit did we learn how intensely brisket is judged. We never heard of some of the terminology used to judge brisket. In the competition circuit, when the judges walk around, they look at how clean your smoke is, but a variety of woods

create different colors of smoke, so when we cook off of charcoal and wood, our smoke isn't clear. Most competitors use fancy gas grills; we stick to open firepits, which are not allowed in most competitions. We learned quickly that the sport of barbeque has become more important than its original purpose, to bring those from all walks of life together to commune over good barbeque food made with love and legacy.

We cook brisket to eat, not for its presentation. We didn't enter the barbeque game for aesthetics; we cook barbeque to feed our community. However, my uncles Aubrey and Stevie always had the mindset that they could compete with anyone. We have always been confident about our barbeque.

Brisket wasn't common in Wilson, but we fed people in Raleigh who wanted to see brisket on our menu. We put our brisket on the smoker, and our pitmasters would do what we call "eyeball cooking," no thermometers or fancy techniques. They cooked the brisket until it was nice and juicy and dashed it with our vinegar sauce. Our method doesn't call for any trimming. Fat is flavor, and you can remove unwanted pieces after the brisket is done.

5 tablespoons coarsely ground black pepper

2 tablespoons coarse kosher salt

2 tablespoons paprika

2 tablespoons date sugar

1 (12- to 14-pound) whole brisket

½ cup Bavarian or yellow mustard

PREHEAT the smoker to 225°F using oak wood and charcoal using the indirect cooking method.

IN a small bowl, stir together the pepper, salt, paprika, and date sugar. Rub the brisket with the mustard and apply the seasoning evenly over all sides of the meat. Place the brisket in the smoker over indirect heat. Close the lid and smoke for 5 hours, or until the internal temperature reaches 165°F.

SPREAD unwaxed butcher paper on your work surface. Remove the brisket from the smoker and place it in the middle of the paper. Wrap the brisket until it is completely enclosed and fold the paper over twice, with the brisket ending right-side (the side with the fat cap) up. The unwaxed paper should be twice the size of the brisket so that you have enough room for the meat to properly cook. Place the wrapped brisket back in the smoker, right-side up, and do not remove it until the brisket reaches an internal temperature of 205°F.

4

RELISHES AND SAUCES

The Tobacco Harvest

For me, barbeque has always been synonymous with happy times. When I was a kid in 1950s Wilson, North Carolina, we barbequed to celebrate our work on the tobacco harvest. It was the only time during my childhood when Blacks and whites ate side by side. Those barbeques are still fixed in my memory because even though racism and prejudice was alive and well back then, I felt for a brief moment that we were colorblind. I still associate barbeque with that time in my life when color, ethnicity, religion, and gender didn't matter. What mattered was that together, we were working on and celebrating something bigger than ourselves.

The tobacco harvest typically took place from mid- to late summer, occasionally spilling into fall. For three summers, starting when I was twelve, I picked tobacco leaves as seasonal help for a local farmer named Mr. Renfow. He owned several large tobacco farms in Wilson County, and every summer he'd come downtown to find laborers, most of whom were African Americans.

My cousins, friends, and I, along with a few strangers, arrived at the farm each morning at 4 a.m. to unload the previous night's smoked tobacco from the curing barn. By 6 a.m., we were working in the fields to twist the ripe tobacco leaves from the plants. The unripe leaves were left on the stalk until they were ready for harvesting days or weeks later. We'd place the cut leaves onto a truck, which would transport them to the curing barn. At the curing barn, the women, who were usually a mix of both Black and white, would loop the tobacco leaves onto tobacco sticks. When the men were done harvesting at the end of the day, they'd head back to the barn to hang the sticks for that evening's cure. Once the barn was full, Mr. Renfow would fire it up, using

local oak to smoke the leaves, oxidizing them into sweet, smooth submission. This was the cure that turned tobacco leaves into a viable consumer product.

At the end of the tobacco harvest, the landowner would treat his staff to a grandiose barbeque. This was a tradition passed down from plantation life, when harvests were so important to the estate that white planters promised sweet cakes and a week off at Christmas for the enslaved if the harvest went well.

The older African American laborers, the ones who worked on Mr. Renfow's farm year-round, were in charge of barbequing the pigs for the end of the tobacco season barbeque. They dug enormous pits, laid sand down to soak up the drippings, chopped the wood, and fired the coals. When the coals were good and hot, they'd splay several just-killed pigs over the fire. Meanwhile, the women were in charge of cooking the sides—collard greens, coleslaw, Brunswick stew, and cornbread. When it was ready, we all sat down at several long tables, wherever we could find a spot, and ate all this delicious food family-style. Fried chicken, lemonade, and sweet tea were also passed around the tables. The barbeque

ended with pineapple upside-down and chocolate cakes.

Whenever there was a barbeque happening in town, anyone could and would stop in. That's just how it was in the South. And since the harvest barbeque was especially big, it meant the entire town was together, Blacks and whites alike. It was a magical moment for a twelve-year-old. Despite all our differences—socioeconomic and racial—it was the time in our life when we sat down and thanked the good Lord for the harvest and the end of a season. Through celebration and barbeque, we saw our commonalities instead of our differences.

Barbeque is an event of celebration. We were fortunate to share something in common. We reaped rewards when the tobacco farm owner sold the crop we harvested. Tobacco supported our region and everyone in it. We did most of the cooking and they did most of the eating. I dream of an equitable North Carolina without the unnecessary hurdles my forebears and I encountered. So many people took what we created and made

millions off it because we didn't have the financial resources, access to education, and support in business. *I, too, sing America.*

AUBREY MITCHELL, middle son of Willie and Doretha Mitchell

Back in the 1970s, when I was a young man, we would make $40 to $60 a week cropping tobacco. We would work up a sweat and want to drink a cold refreshment and eat during our work hours. The store near the tobacco factory would credit your account and take what you owed for whatever you spent on snacks and drinks during the workweek at the tobacco factory out of your paycheck. It was better to bring your own snacks and drinks, or your check at the end of the week would make you cry. I can even remember when my friend and I were hired to pick cucumbers. We left the house when it was still dark, jumped on the back of the truck, and came back home when it was dark again. We made $6 each for an entire day of picking cucumbers. We didn't pick cucumbers for long.

THE CITY OF WILSON, NORTH CAROLINA, was founded in 1849. Tobacco built Wilson. In 1890, the first tobacco warehouse opened in town. Tobacco was a major cash crop, and Wilson was once known for being the "Largest Tobacco Market in the World." By 1888, the Knights of Labor, one of the largest labor organizations in the United States, began to organize tobacco workers in Wilson. However, during the Jim Crow era, African Americans continued to be underpaid, overworked, and underrepresented. By the 1940s, Black tobacco workers organized to fight for their civil rights and protest labor injustices in Eastern North Carolina tobacco factories. According to the *Pittsburgh Courier*, in 1940, two large tobacco companies were fined $32,000 "for underpaying Negro tobacco stemmers." African Americans were the majority laborers in tobacco warehouses during the tobacco boom. Throughout the nineteenth and twentieth centuries, corporate tobacco companies not only exploited African American tobacco laborers but also used stereotypical images of African Americans to sell and market their products.

TOBACCO FARM IN 1944

BRASWELL PLANTATION BATTLEBORO, NORTH CAROLINA

PHOTO NO. 4518

Sir Walter Raleigh, a sixteenth-century Roanoke colonist, documented Indigenous communities growing tobacco for medicinal, ceremonial, and personal use. The colonists would later mass produce tobacco that would become a major cash crop of the Carolinas. In 1839, an enslaved man named Stephen accidentally discovered a curing process that created the bright leaf tobacco that is used today in cigarettes. This multibillion dollar industry created tremendous wealth and jobs for many including citizens of Wilson, North Carolina, where tobacco was in production 24 hours a day. Although, the legacy of tobacco for African Americans, Indigenous, and working class whites reveals a turbulent past.

Ed's Eastern North Carolina Vinegar BBQ Sauce

Serves 12 • **Prep Time:** 15 minutes • **Cooking Time:** 10 minutes

My mother taught me how to make our vinegar barbeque sauce. I can still remember the smell of the tangy sauce boiling on our stove when I was a child. In Eastern North Carolina, there are two styles of whole-hog barbeque: The first is the festive pig pickin', where a barbequed pig that's been slathered with sauce is set on a bar and people pick off what they want. The second is when the whole hog is chopped—the meat is pulled from the bones and skin, the skin is toasted into cracklin', and the meat and cracklin' are then chopped up and seasoned.

> I RECEIVED MY CULINARY DEGREE FROM MOTHER DORETHA'S UNIVERSITY.
>
> —Ed Mitchell

The same ingredients—cider vinegar, brown sugar, salt, black pepper, and red pepper flakes—are used to season both styles of whole-hog barbeque. However, for the pig pickin', the sauce is mopped on the pig during the final hour of cooking. For the chopped barbeque, the sauce ingredients are added to the meat one at a time, just before serving. We recommend using this sauce to season whole hogs for a pig pickin', barbequed whole turkey, or baby back ribs. It makes about 1 gallon of sauce, enough to season one 150-pound hog, three 18- to 20-pound turkeys, or 8 racks of ribs.

1 gallon apple cider vinegar

1 cup red pepper flakes, plus more if needed

1 cup packed dark brown sugar, plus more if needed

1 cup hot sauce (True Made Foods Cayenne Hot Sauce), plus more if needed

½ cup smoked paprika

¼ cup kosher salt, plus more if needed

2 tablespoons freshly ground black pepper

1 tablespoon minced garlic

COMBINE all the ingredients in a container and stir until the sugar has dissolved. Taste and add more salt, red pepper flakes, hot sauce, or brown sugar to suit you. Just before applying, strain the sauce through a fine-mesh sieve.

Doretha's Gravy: "Ain't That Gravy Good!"

Serves 3 • **Prep Time:** 6 minutes • **Cooking Time:** 10 minutes

MAMA MITCHELL, DORETHA MITCHELL, 91 years old

Brown your flour in the oil drippings from whatever meat you fried, or you can make gravy just from lard and flour. Add your salt, pepper, onion, and garlic. Add water, stir, and let it thicken. Do not leave the gravy unattended. Cook for 5 to 10 minutes on low-medium heat. It's easy. Season to your taste. Pour the gravy over rice, chicken, or pork chops.

2 tablespoons lard

1 cup of all-purpose flour

¼ cup of water

2 garlic cloves, minced

¼ cup minced yellow onion

1 teaspoon sugar

Salt and freshly ground black pepper

Biscuits or cooked white rice, for serving

IN a medium saucepan, melt the lard over low-medium heat. Add the flour and whisk continuously for about 4 minutes, until the flour browns. Make sure that the flour doesn't stick; add a little water if need be. Add the garlic, onion, sugar, and salt and pepper to taste. Whisk for an additional 2 minutes. Serve with biscuits or over white rice.

Hellwig Bacon-Tomato Jam

Serves 6 • **Prep Time:** 15 minutes • **Cooking Time:** 1 hour

Bacon-tomato jam was a popular menu item for our Raleigh customers, created by our sous chef John Hellwig, a culinary genius. John makes the most incredible side dishes and appetizers. He was able to reimagine the side dishes we ate at home as beautiful menu items. John has been with us for fifteen years. He was the first creative mind that I allowed to give a city twist to Southern classics.

1 pound thick-cut bacon, cooked and chopped

1 yellow onion, diced

2 garlic cloves, minced

½ cup pure molasses

¼ cup apple cider vinegar

1½ tablespoons yellow mustard

1 cup diced tomatoes

1 tablespoon light brown sugar

½ teaspoon red pepper flakes

¼ teaspoon freshly ground black pepper

Biscuits, for serving

IN a medium cast-iron skillet or saucepan, cook the bacon over medium heat until golden brown, about 7 minutes. Add the onion and garlic, and cook until the onion is caramelized and translucent. Add the molasses, vinegar, mustard, tomatoes, sugar, red pepper flakes, and black pepper and simmer on low, stirring occasionally, for about 45 minutes, until the mixture thickens. Remove from the heat and let cool for 5 minutes, then transfer the bacon jam to a food processor and pulse on low for 3 minutes. Transfer the bacon jam to a mason jar. Store in the refrigerator for up to 2 days. Serve with buttery biscuits.

Toisnot Tartar Sauce

Serves 4 • **Prep Time:** 8 minutes

Toisnot Park is a popular recreation area on the east side of Wilson, a gathering place with a lake and a softball field. The name derives from Tosneoc, a word from the Tuscarora Iroquoian language meaning "close to two rivers." The Tuscarora were the earliest inhabitants of Wilson County. They lived off the land and our rivers. Later, Wilmington residents brought their love of seafood culture from the coast to Wilson.

Today, Wilson is known for barbeque and tobacco, but Wilson County once had an abundance of freshwater fish. For many Black, Indigenous, and impoverished people, fishing was survival. Fishing in the surrounding lakes, creeks, and rivers would feed a family for a few days. Fishing was also a huge part of the Mitchell tradition. As a family, we didn't hunt that much, but fishing was bonding time and therapy for the men in our family.

Our Toisnot Tartar Sauce is served with Southern Fried Fish and Home Fries (page 122).

1 cup mayonnaise (preferably Duke's)

½ cup diced dill pickle

2 tablespoons chopped fresh dill

1 teaspoon fresh lemon juice

1 teaspoon garlic powder

1 teaspoon salt

MIX all the ingredients in a medium bowl. Cover and chill in the refrigerator for at least an hour before serving.

5

BISCUITS AND CORNBREAD

Rites of Passage

When we cooked barbeque, the men would stay up all night, playing music on their guitars and drinking moonshine. That moonshine jug would be passed around as the fire was brewing.

In the old days, hogs were barbequed in the ground, then, later, in barrels. We built brick pits aboveground in our restaurant, which has the same effect as barbequing hogs in the ground. I was the first one in Wilson County to build aboveground indoor pits.

I am a traditionalist. Whole-hog barbeque is labor-intensive, but it is the original art form of barbeque. Barbequing a whole hog to perfection means mastering the art and science behind cooking the fattier and leaner cuts of the hog all at once.

Hoop Cheese Biscuits

Serves 8 • **Prep Time:** 10 minutes • **Cooking Time:** 12 to 15 minutes

MAMA MITCHELL, DORETHA MITCHELL, 91 years old

I make my biscuits with North Carolina hoop cheese. You can also use smoked Gouda cheese. Make sure you always use quality ingredients, including self-rising flour. You have to sift your flour. Sifting your flour makes your biscuits light and airy.

Add the cheese to the flour once the dough is at a medium consistency. Bake the biscuits until they are a light golden brown color. I like lard with my biscuits. Lard has the flavor in it. You don't want your biscuits too greasy. Just a touch of love. Take your time when you cook. There is no rush. Cooking is art, and you have to want to do it. We should all want to eat good food with our family. Look at my children and how big they are.

Vegetable oil

2½ cups sifted self-rising flour, plus more for dusting

1 cup grated North Carolina hoop or smoked Gouda cheese

¾ cup buttermilk, plus more if needed

2 tablespoons lard, or 4 tablespoons (½ stick) unsalted butter

PREHEAT your oven to 450°F. Oil a baking sheet.

IN a medium bowl, combine 2 cups of the self-rising flour, the cheese, the buttermilk, and the lard. Mix the dough together with your hands or with an electric or handheld mixer. Add more buttermilk if needed to achieve the correct dough consistency. Flour a clean work surface and roll out the dough with a floured rolling pin to a medium thickness. Cut the dough with a standard biscuit cutter. Place the cut biscuits on the prepared baking sheet. Bake for 12 to 15 minutes, until the biscuits are golden brown.

Silver Dollar Corn Cakes with Smoked Honey Butter

Serves 3 to 5 • **Prep Time:** 15 minutes • **Cooking Time:** 20 minutes

These corn cakes are to beans and barbeque what tortilla chips are to salsa and guacamole—the perfect vessel for scooping up food. We source our bourbon-infused honey from a local beekeeper at Garden Supply Company in Cary, North Carolina. If you can't find it, mix a few drops of good bourbon, like Woodford Reserve Single Barrel, into your favorite honey. These silver dollar corn cakes will have you licking your fingers, savoring every bite.

Smoked Honey Butter:

1 cup unsalted butter, softened

1 teaspoon paprika

1 teaspoon freshly ground black pepper

1 teaspoon salt

1 teaspoon garlic powder

⅓ cup bourbon-infused honey (see directions below)

¼ cup confectioners' sugar

½ teaspoon freshly ground nutmeg

Corn Cakes:

1 cup old-fashioned stone-ground cornmeal

1 cup self-rising flour

⅓ cup packed dark brown sugar

½ teaspoon fine salt

2 large eggs

1 cup almond milk or oat milk

⅓ cup cold water

2 tablespoons light molasses (not blackstrap or robust)

¼ to ½ cup vegetable oil

Hot honey or molasses, for serving

PREHEAT your smoker to 200°F with oak or pecan wood chips.

MAKE the smoked honey butter: In a medium stainless-steel bowl, combine the butter, paprika, pepper, salt, and garlic powder. Add the bourbon-infused honey (one shot of a good bourbon, and 1 tablespoon of honey). Mix the butter. Put the bowl on the grill and smoke the butter for 8 minutes. Do not let the butter scorch. Let the butter cool for 3 minutes. Add the confectioners' sugar and nutmeg. Mix with a spoon or an electric mixer. Let cool at room temperature until the butter solidifies. Cover and store in the refrigerator for no more than 2 days.

MAKE the corn cakes: In a large bowl, whisk together the cornmeal, flour, brown sugar, and salt. In a medium bowl, beat the eggs. Whisk in the almond milk, water, and molasses until blended. Stir the wet ingredients into the dry ingredients until just combined.

HEAT a large, heavy-bottomed skillet over medium heat. Once hot, add just enough vegetable oil to coat the pan, 1 to 2 tablespoons. When the oil shimmers, drop the batter by 1 full teaspoon into the skillet for true silver dollar–sized corn cakes. Sear each corn cake on the first side until light golden brown, 1 to 2 minutes. Using a metal spatula, flip the cakes and cook until light golden brown on the second side, about 1 minute more. Drain the corn cakes on paper towels. Repeat until all the batter has been cooked, adding oil to coat the pan between batches. Serve the corn cakes with the smoked honey butter and hot honey or molasses.

Classic Skillet Cornbread

Serves 3 to 6 • **Prep Time:** 10 minutes • **Cooking Time:** 15 minutes

My mother would make fried johnnycakes and serve them with fried sea mullet and shrimp. When I was growing up, she would make flour bread with molasses and peanut butter with a little fatback and a side dish of slow-cooked pinto beans. The old folks know about how good that was; it was mouthwatering. We always served classic skillet cornbread at our restaurant to give them a taste of our mama's kitchen.

2 cups coarse stone-ground yellow cornmeal

½ cup self-rising flour, sifted

2 tablespoons sugar

1½ teaspoons salt

2 medium-sized eggs

1¼ cups buttermilk

¾ cup (1½ sticks) salted butter, melted, plus butter for serving

2 tablespoons lard or butter

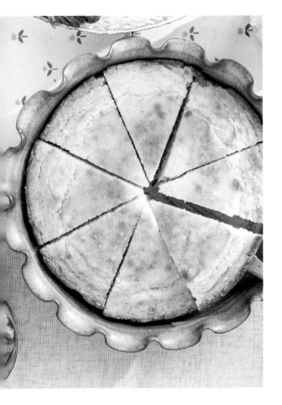

PREHEAT your oven to 400°F. While you are mixing the cornbread, warm a 10-inch cast-iron skillet in the oven.

IN a large bowl, mix cornmeal, flour, sugar, salt, and eggs. In another bowl, mix the buttermilk and the melted butter. Add the wet ingredients to the dry ingredients and stir to combine. Set aside.

CAREFULLY remove the hot cast-iron skillet from the oven. Over medium-low heat, melt the lard in the skillet. Add the cornmeal batter and cook for 2 to 3 minutes, then carefully transfer the skillet to the oven and bake the cornbread for 20 minutes. Stick a long toothpick into the center of the cornbread; the cornbread is done if the toothpick comes out clean. Take a slice of butter and spread it all over the top of the cornbread.

6

SALADS AND SLAW

War, Peace, and Jim Crow: Barbequing with My Brothers

I LOST NAT'S SWINGING BODY IN A RAIN OF TEARS AND HEARD MY SON SCREAM ALL THE WAY FROM ANZIO FOR PEACE HE NEVER KNEW . . . I LEARNED DA NANG AND PORK CHOP HILL IN ANGUISH.

—Mari Evans, "I Am a Black Woman"

I was drafted to serve in Vietnam while I was attending Fayetteville State University. I wasn't supposed to be drafted, because I was enrolled in college and playing football. They drafted me anyway. I was so close to finishing my business and sociology degree. For Black men at that time, careers in education or politics were our only options. I was studying to become a high school principal. The local board started drafting young Black men in college to fill their quota, even though it was against the law. My college sent the local draft board proof that I was enrolled in college, but they used a loophole to draft me. According to the draft board, I wasn't enrolled for both semesters that year, even though enrollment for the next semester hadn't started yet.

I was drafted into the army as a junior private and stationed at Fort Bragg; later, I was sent to Fort Benning in Georgia. I was twenty-four years old when I was shipped off to Da Nang, Vietnam. I will never forget when my platoon was ordered to protect a stronghold at the Marble Mountains in Vietnam. We were bombed every night and were under a barrage of mortar attacks. The nine recruits who were there before me were killed. I try to wipe those memories away. The only good memory I have of the Vietnam War is the brotherhood. It was the only time race, class, and gender didn't matter. We were all in it together.

My parents mailed me recorded tapes of their voices via the Red Cross. I cherished every tape that arrived. So many young men were being killed so quickly. Our brothers, cousins, neighbors, and friends of mine were being killed every day. It really shook my mother and father to their core. I served in Vietnam for eighteen months. Every day, I longed for my mom's good cooking. When I came home, my entire family, friends, and neighbors had a huge pig pickin' waiting for me.

AUBREY MITCHELL, middle son of Willie and Doretha Mitchell

I cried all the time. My parents would hear about young men getting killed. We were always on edge. We would hear our parents crying and praying. It was a lot for us because my brother Stevie and I were ten years younger. Our cousin Gaskin was going to join Ed's platoon. He jumped out of a plane and was shot dead immediately. It was an eerie time. We never knew when we would get that call. We were so grateful that Ed had every arm and leg and his mind was still intact when he came home. That was a blessing in itself, and we thank God, because there were so many who didn't make it back. What I remember most was the feast we had when he came home. My parents' firstborn son was home, and they made sure they fed him well. I still don't understand how he was drafted—he was going to college and playing football.

They still took him from us.

OFTENTIMES, mainstream history and Hollywood omits the history of Black soldiers in Vietnam. Wallace Terry was the first African American journalist at *Time* magazine to cover the Vietnam War. In 1967, *Time*'s Washington bureau flew Terry to Saigon to cover a story on the role of Black soldiers in the war. The Vietnam War was the first war in which African Americans were fully integrated in combat and held positions of leadership in the military. Although the White House praised the valiant courage of America's Black soldiers, they were dying in combat at an alarming rate. By 1967, Black soldiers made up 16.3 percent of those drafted and 23 percent of combat troops, yet Black people accounted for only 11 percent of the total US population. In 1984, Terry published *Bloods: Black Veterans of the Vietnam War: An Oral History*, based on his interviews with Black soldiers during the war. *Bloods* became one of the most significant glimpses of the Black experience during the Vietnam War. Almost sixty years later, it remains the definitive account documenting the stories of African American soldiers' service in Vietnam. Spike Lee's 2020 movie *Da 5 Bloods* was based on Terry's book. Ed Mitchell and a generation of young Black men were disproportionately drafted in comparison to their white counterparts. For Ed Mitchell, barbeque also became therapeutic.

Blue Cheese Wedge Salad with BBQ Chicken

Serves 2 • **Prep Time:** 8 minutes, plus 1 hour chilling

Blue cheese wedge salad was another John Hellwig creation, and one of our most popular menu items among our Raleigh patrons. Our restaurant in Wilson was a service-line style of restaurant, and once we moved to seated service in Raleigh, we started to offer appetizers. That was new for us. The wedge salad gave us an opportunity to be economical and add our barbequed meat in a creative way. Wedge salads were not common in barbeque restaurants. We took pride in reimagining barbeque without losing the flavor and tradition. We would garnish our wedge salads with smoked pork, chicken, brisket, or tofu.

1 green onion, diced

½ cup buttermilk

½ cup mayonnaise

½ cup (4 ounces) sour cream

1 tablespoon lemon juice or white wine vinegar

1 cup crumbled blue cheese

1 teaspoon garlic powder

Sea salt and freshly ground black pepper

1 head iceberg lettuce, quartered

1 cup diced barbequed chicken

IN a medium bowl, combine the green onion, buttermilk, mayonnaise, sour cream, lemon juice, blue cheese, garlic powder, and a dash each of salt and pepper. Cover with plastic wrap and refrigerate the salad dressing for 1 hour. Top each lettuce wedge with barbequed chicken and some blue cheese dressing.

In My Grandmother's Garden: Cucumber Salad

Serves 4 to 6 • **Prep Time:** 15 minutes

RYAN MITCHELL, Ed Mitchell's son

Cucumbers grew in my grandmother's garden. We didn't have to go out and buy a lot of our vegetables. We always had cucumbers. Grandmother would make a cucumber salad, or we would eat them semi-pickled and dip them in our vinegar sauce. I think about how so many perceive our food as "slave food" or unhealthy food, and I can't help but shake my head in disagreement. Since I was a child, we always ate vegetables straight from the garden or the farm.

At the 1995 Source Awards, André 3000, of the Southern hip-hop group OutKast, said, "The South got something to say." I would say we still have something to say, but this time, it's about our food and culinary legacy. Matriarchs like my grandmother didn't use canned vegetables—everything was made from scratch, and they knew how to feed an army with basic food staples.

1½ cups white wine vinegar

2 teaspoons honey

1 tablespoon chopped fresh dill

1 teaspoon Italian seasoning

Salt and freshly ground black pepper

2 farmer's market English (seedless) cucumbers

⅓ cup diced red onion

COMBINE the vinegar, honey, dill, Italian seasoning, and salt and pepper to taste in a large bowl. Add the cucumbers and red onion. Refrigerate for a few hours, then serve.

Ed's Shindig Slaw

Serves 8 • **Prep Time:** 15 minutes

As with barbeque sauce, coleslaws from the eastern and western sides of North Carolina are very different. The west's Lexington "red slaw," which replaces mayo with ketchup, uses the same ingredients as their ketchup-based barbeque sauce, but in slightly different proportions. It's a red-tinted sweet-and-sour sauce with no mayonnaise.

The eastern part of the state combines its sugar-and-vinegar-based barbeque sauce with only sliced cabbage (no carrots or onions). I, however, happen to like the taste and color of carrots. I also like mayonnaise in my slaw—its creaminess complements the vinegar's acidity and suits a plate of barbeque beautifully. This is neither eastern nor western coleslaw. It's coleslaw my way.

Notes: Duke's is the mayonnaise of choice in many parts of the South, and is the preferred mayonnaise in North Carolina. It tastes close to a homemade mayonnaise—smooth and sweet, with a tangy jolt on the finish. If you can't find Duke's, we also like Miracle Whip. Use a food processor or fine grater to shred the cabbage, if you prefer.

1 small head green cabbage (about 2 pounds)

2 or 3 medium carrots

Salt

1 cup mayonnaise (preferably Duke's; see Notes)

2 tablespoons sugar

2 tablespoons white wine vinegar

1 tablespoon red wine vinegar

2 teaspoons yellow mustard

Freshly ground black pepper

QUARTER the cabbage through its core. Cut out and discard the core, then cut the cabbage crosswise into ¼-inch-thick slices (see Notes) and place in a large bowl. Using the large holes of a cheese grater, grate the carrots on an angle into long strands. Toss the carrots with the cabbage. Sprinkle generously with salt (so it looks like there's been a light snowfall), toss to mix, and let sit for a few minutes.

MEANWHILE, in a medium bowl, mix the mayonnaise, sugar, vinegars, mustard, and a big pinch each of salt and pepper until combined. Add the mayonnaise mixture to the cabbage and carrots and toss to coat. Taste the slaw. Does it need more acidity? If so, add a little more vinegar. Does it need more spice? Add a little more pepper. If it doesn't taste delicious yet, it needs more salt. Chill for at least 30 minutes before serving.

"I Don't Eat Everybody's Potato Salad!"

Serves 5 • **Prep Time:** 20 to 25 minutes • **Cooking Time:** 12 to 15 minutes

RYAN MITCHELL, Ed Mitchell's son

Suggs Christian Temple is the name of our home church in Wilson. My grandparents were cofounders of the church, and their names are still on the church walls. Granddad co-owned the land and gave it to the church to be built in 1978. For the Mitchells, church on Sunday was law in our family. All of us went to church, even my grandfather. Church for me was the best time to see all my friends. The Sunday service was always good, but to play with all the kids from my church in the park next door was the highlight of my childhood. The food and the hospitality that went into post-church was so amazing to me.

Every First Sunday, we partook of bread and wine, and we would commune by washing one another's feet. A lot of Black churches have moved away from that tradition.

We washed one another's feet up until the late 1990s. It was an act of service, humbling yourself in front of your neighbors. The women washed one another's feet, and vice versa with the men. They were country boys who didn't put on shoes until Sunday. You can't re-create that kind of humility today; you have to believe in that type of community service based in scripture. I sat next to my granddad so that we could wash each other's feet. Granddad would say, "We understand the service, but my baby ain't going to be washing everybody's feet, y'all could chill with that." It was the smelliest and best of times.

Reverend Denmark Suggs was our original pastor. Our church pastor's anniversary dinner was held every year, and this is when Reverend Suggs would ask my grandmother to make the potato salad. Only a select few church members were asked to make the potato salad. First Sunday, my grandmother would always

cook for our fellow parishioners. She always made sure our favorite dishes were on the menu so that she wouldn't have to cook for us after church.

So when we say "I don't eat everybody's potato salad" in the Black community, that means either the person didn't know how to season or prepare potato salad in the old way, or their home was unclean. I recall older Black women at church saying, "She might have all kinds of stuff in her house. I don't know if I want to eat her potato salad." As a child, you hear all the gossip at church.

Reverend Suggs always visited our house. My grandfather and he were fishing buddies. Pastor knew how clean my grandmother's house was and that her kitchen was always spotless. You could eat off the floor in my grandmother's house, and my grandmother's potato salad was legendary. We served it at our restaurant, pig pickin's, church, and every family function.

5 pounds russet potatoes

1½ cups regular mayonnaise (preferably Duke's)

¼ cup yellow mustard

4 green onions, diced

1 teaspoon kosher salt

½ teaspoon freshly ground black pepper

5 small sweet pickles, diced

4 hard-boiled eggs, diced

4 slices bacon, cooked and crumbled

1 teaspoon paprika

WRAP the potatoes in aluminum foil. Place the potatoes on the smoker and cook for 30 minutes. Take the hot potatoes from the smoker, let cool, and remove the potato skins with peeler. Put the potatoes in a bowl and mash or whip them to make them extra fluffy. Fold in the mayonnaise, mustard, green onions, salt, pepper, and your favorite seasonings. Fold in the pickles, eggs, and bacon, then adjust the seasoning, adding more salt, mustard, or mayo as needed. Refrigerate for 15 minutes before serving. Lightly garnish with the paprika just before serving.

7

POULTRY, SEAFOOD, AND TOFU

Mastering the Art of Barbeque with Mr. Kirby

Growing up, most everyone in Wilson cooked barbeque in their own backyard. Everybody had a homemade pit. It was routine, the norm for us back then. Cooking barbeque was part of Black Wilson's lifestyle and culture. There were two men in my neighborhood who knew how to really cook good barbeque and make moonshine, Mr. James Kirby and Sam Morgan. Mr. Kirby taught me a technique called banking the coals (see page 9), showing me how to position the coals around the hog so the meat would cook to perfection. He even taught me some techniques that my dad didn't know.

Mr. Kirby was a quiet man. He didn't do a lot of talking. He just did what needed to be done. You just had to follow his lead. I was determined to learn from Mr. Kirby. One day he asked me, "Do you really want to learn how to cook barbeque?" I said, "Yeah, I really want to learn." He repeated himself and then asked me for a third and then a fourth time. I got a little irritated and said loudly, "Yes, I want to learn!"

I was in my early twenties. Mr. Kirby said, "Well, if you really want to learn, I will put you in the water, but it's up to you to learn how to swim." I said, "You put me in the water and I will swim!" I tagged along with him every time he cooked barbeque. I would bring my sandwich and sodas and sit around the fire waiting for Mr. Kirby to show up.

He showed up and got the coals real hot and then positioned them around the hog and got the temperature up to 400° to 500°F. Then he shut off the vents and the exhaust system. He closed the lid, picked up his jacket, and walked off. I was stunned, just watching him walk away from the pit. I said, "Where are you going, Mr. Kirby?"

He said, "I'm going home."

I said, "Who is going to watch the pig?"

He said, "You can sit here all night if you want to."

What he was doing was testing me in learning the trade. I was scared to death thinking we were going to burn the hog. I couldn't wait to get there in the morning to check on it. I just knew the pig was going to burn. I was tossing and turning all night. I woke up at 4:30 a.m. to check on the hog. I raised the lid, and it was the most beautiful caramel-colored pig I had ever seen. It amazed and surprised me. I was humbled to learn that technique. Most people think you have to stay up all night barbequing a hog. You don't have to do that all night if your skill set is good.

IN 1907, the Raleigh *News & Observer* reported the murder of a Wilson barbeque legend, Robert Hilliard. Hilliard, an African American sharecropper, was operating a "barbeque stand" on the "Owens Place," a white landowner's property in Wilson on Saratoga Road. The article states that Hilliard "did a thriving business selling barbeque and sandwiches until two o'clock." During the wee hours of the night, at the "dance and barbeque supper," Hilliard was murdered by an irate customer named Will Scarborough. This archival news clip is one of the earliest records of a barbeque business operated by an African American in Wilson. According to *Race and Politics in North Carolina, 1872–1901* by Eric Anderson, in 1910, Wilson County had the state's second lowest percentage of Black ownership of farmland, at 0.5 percent per capita, in comparison to Bertie County, which had the highest, at 3.1 percent. During the Jim Crow era, African Americans had limited opportunities and oftentimes were restricted from owning land and becoming business owners. Robert Hilliard was one Black entrepreneur who defied the odds and was able to start his own barbeque stand on the Owens property. However, it is unclear how much profit Hilliard made from the barbeque stand. Throughout the nineteenth and twentieth centuries, Black pitmasters operated many barbeque stands throughout the Carolinas, but only a small number owned their stands.

Doretha's Fried Chicken

Serves 5 • **Prep Time:** 15 minutes • **Cooking Time:** 20 minutes

Mama was one of thirty-six children, and each one of her siblings had seven or eight children themselves. A running joke in Wilson is that everyone is cousins. Fried chicken fed large families, and many families raised their own chickens. I remember my mama's fried chicken before people starting buying packaged processed chickens in supermarkets. I will never forget the taste of farm-raised chicken; the meat was so juicy. She learned how to make fried chicken from my grandmother Beatrice. When we were little, we would go to our grandmother's house, and her chicken and biscuits would be on a platter covered with a tea cloth on the stove. Even after we would play for hours and come inside our grandmother's home, those chicken and biscuits were still kicking.

RYAN MITCHELL, Ed Mitchell's son

I remember the cast-iron skillet. My grandmother was meticulous about cleaning chicken. She washed the chicken for hours before she fried it. I always thought that's why it tasted so good. Growing up, her chicken was thoroughly cleaned, seasoned well, and dry battered straight into a hot frying pan. The skin was a beautiful golden bronze. It wasn't overly crunchy. Grandmother's chicken was still crispy three days later in the refrigerator. I think my grandmother's generation had better ingredients; processing food has changed a lot of the flavor of food. We do our best to bring the flavor of the past to our customers.

¼ cup honey

½ teaspoon cayenne pepper

4 teaspoons hot smoked paprika

2 tablespoons plus 1½ teaspoons kosher salt

1 cup buttermilk

2 garlic cloves, minced

2 teaspoons ground sage

2 teaspoons freshly ground black pepper

1 whole chicken (farm-raised is the best), washed then cut into 8 pieces

1 cup all-purpose flour

2 tablespoons cornstarch

Canola oil or lard, for frying

IN a small bowl, whisk together the honey, cayenne, 1 teaspoon of the paprika, and ½ teaspoon salt. Cover the bowl and set it aside at room temperature. In another small bowl, whisk together the buttermilk, garlic, remaining 3 teaspoons paprika, 2 tablespoons salt, sage, and black pepper. Pour the buttermilk mixture into a large resealable plastic bag and add the chicken. Close the bag and shake thoroughly to coat the chicken. Refrigerate the chicken for at least 4 hours or preferably overnight.

TAKE the chicken out of the refrigerator 1 hour before you're ready to cook it so it can come to room temperature. In a large baking dish, whisk together the flour, cornstarch, and 1 teaspoon salt.

FILL a large cast-iron skillet about halfway with oil and heat over medium-high heat. Working with one piece at a time, remove the chicken from the bag, allowing the excess buttermilk to drip back into the bag, and place the chicken in the flour mixture. Dredge each piece lightly to coat on all sides and transfer to a plate. Discard the excess buttermilk and flour mixtures.

ONCE the oil is at medium heat, working in batches of four, use tongs to place the chicken in the skillet. Cook the chicken, turning the pieces every few minutes and adjusting the heat as needed, until the skin is golden brown and the chicken is 175°F internally.

PLATE the chicken and drizzle with the honey mix.

Barbequed Spatchcocked Chicken

Serves 4 • **Prep Time:** 30 minutes, plus marinating overnight • **Cooking Time:** 1 hour

My mother's barbequed chicken was actually a mix of baked and barbequed. Mama would always serve barbequed chicken with white rice. The oven drippings from her barbequed chicken were used as a light gravy over our rice. Those old-school speckled-black-and-white enameled roasting pans bring back so many memories. She would remove the lid off the chicken at the right moment and the skin would turn crispy golden brown.

About 2 cups water

1 cup unsweetened grapefruit juice

½ cup packed brown sugar

¼ cup apple cider vinegar

¼ cup kosher salt

¼ cup freshly ground black pepper

1 tablespoon cayenne pepper

1 whole chicken, spatchcocked

¼ cup Bavarian mustard

True Made Foods Ed's "Mother of All" Spice Rub

True Made Foods Ed's Kansas City BBQ Sauce, for serving

IN a bowl or tub large enough to hold a whole chicken, mix the water, grapefruit juice, brown sugar, vinegar, salt, black pepper, and cayenne and stir until the sugar and salt have dissolved. Add the whole chicken and submerge it in the brine. Refrigerate for 8 hours.

PREHEAT the oven to 400°F.

REMOVE the chicken from the brine and pat dry (discard the brine). Using kitchen shears, split the chicken spatchcock-style, cutting down the ribs. The wings should be sticking up toward you and the breast should be down. Slather with the mustard to coat on both sides, then cover the whole chicken evenly with dry rub. Place breast-side down in a baking pan and cover with aluminum foil.

ROAST on the bottom rack of the oven for about 1 hour, removing the foil from the pan after 30 minutes. Serve with BBQ sauce.

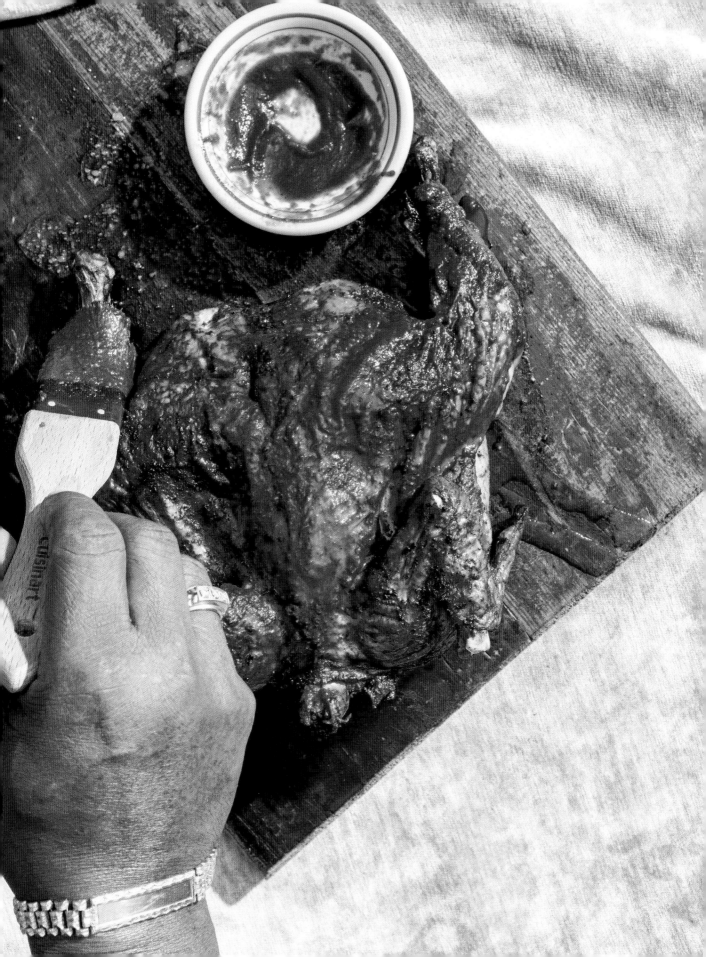

FSU Chicken Pastry

Serves 3 to 5 • **Prep Time:** 30 minutes • **Cooking Time:** 1½ hours

When I attended Fayetteville State University in the 1960s, there was a mom-and-pop restaurant near campus that made chicken pastry similar to my mama's. Chicken pastry is a classic Eastern North Carolina dish made in many homes. My friends and I all ate at that restaurant often and before we would hitch a ride to go back to Wilson on breaks.

RYAN MITCHELL, Ed Mitchell's son

This is one of my grandmother's love-language dishes and a classic North Carolina recipe. I don't know many who make chicken pastry like my grandmother. She made it from scratch every time. Dishes that take a lot of labor and love can be therapeutic. They are a form of art, based on skill and legacy.

I remember my grandmother rolling out dough on her kitchen countertop to make the pastry. It was a Sunday classic, especially in the cooler months. She would top it with thinly sliced boiled eggs. It was so good. When you see someone taking their time to cook something, you associate it with love. When you watch an elder or grandparent cooking, you realize how to make a special dish. A lot of people don't put boiled eggs in

their chicken pastry, but my grandmother would, and she would sprinkle a little black pepper on top. It was always gone in 60 seconds. Most people make their pastry too thick, but my grandmother would roll the dough really thin, almost as thin as a dime.

1 whole chicken, quartered, washed, and skin removed

1 medium yellow onion, diced

2 celery stalks, diced

1 tablespoon salt, plus more as needed

2 whole cloves, ground in a spice grinder

1 bay leaf

8 cups cold water, plus more as needed

3 tablespoons unsalted butter

2 teaspoons freshly ground black pepper, plus more as needed

4 hard-boiled eggs

For the Pastry

2 cups all-purpose flour, plus more for dusting

⅔ cup cold water

1 teaspoon baking powder

¼ cup lard or shortening

IN a large pot, combine the chicken, onion, celery, salt, cloves, bay leaf, and cold water, adding more water if needed to cover the chicken. Bring to a boil, then reduce the heat to low heat. Cover and cook until the chicken is tender, about 45 minutes. Remove the chicken from the pot. Discard the bay leaf, leaving the broth to simmer over low heat. Debone the chicken and cut the meat into small pieces.

IN a large bowl, whisk together the flour, ⅔ cup cold water, and baking powder. Using a pastry cutter, cut in the lard until a coarse dough forms.

LIGHTLY flour a pastry board and roll out the dough until it is a thin layer. Cut the dough into 2-inch strips, then into 2-inch squares.

BRING the broth back to a rolling boil. Drop in the pastry squares, one at a time. Add the butter and pepper to the broth. Once all the pastry has been added, reduce the heat to low medium heat and simmer, uncovered, for 20 minutes. Return the chicken meat to the broth and simmer for 10 minutes more. Slice the boiled eggs and add them to the pot. Simmer for 3 minutes more, cover, and serve hot. Add salt and pepper to taste.

Bougie Barbequed Whole Turkey

Serves 10 • **Prep Time:** 30 minutes • **Cooking Time:** 2 hours

My mother developed this barbequed whole turkey years ago so that our relatives who don't eat pork (and there are a few) could still enjoy good barbeque. Remember that I have twenty-six aunts and uncles just on my mother's side, so family gatherings mean pleasing many different palates. Turkey barbeque became so popular in our house that I started serving it at my restaurant.

Take note that when smoking poultry, the meat and juices may look pink even when the meat is fully cooked. This happens when the pH of the protein is high (or alkaline). When it's low (or acidic), the color of the meat will turn white and the juices will run clear, even if the meat is not safely cooked. Therefore, looking at the juices alone won't tell you if the meat is done; a working meat thermometer that reaches at least 180°F will.

Smoke also creates chemical reactions that make proteins pink. Some pitmasters pride themselves on these reddish-pink smoke rings. While a thermometer is essential, learning to feel meat for doneness with your hands is helpful, too. With poultry, when the bones pull easily from their joints, you're there.

1 (18- to 20-pound) whole turkey

Salt and freshly ground black pepper

1 to 2 cups True Made Foods Ed's Eastern North Carolina Vinegar Barbeque Sauce (page 74)

Potato buns or silver dollar corn cakes (see page 87), for serving

Coleslaw (see page 98), for serving

PREPARE a grill for smoking the turkey. Preheat the smoker to between 225° and 250°F. Place the coals to one side of your smoker. Once hot, place hickory wood chunks on the hot, gray-white charcoals. Set the cooking grate over the fire.

MEANWHILE, butterfly the turkey by splitting it along the backbone, but keep it attached at the breastbone. Flatten it by pressing down on the breastbone with both hands, putting your body weight behind it. Liberally season the turkey on both sides with salt and pepper, so that it looks like a light snow fell on it. Lay it out, skin-side up, on the cooking grate on the side opposite the coals (not directly over them). Cover the grill, adjusting the vents to keep the temperature low, and cook the turkey for 2 hours. Flip the bird so that it's skin-side down and cook until a thermometer inserted into the thickest part of a thigh registers 180°F and the leg bone can easily be tugged from its joint, 45 to 60 minutes more. (If the coals burn down, add more as needed.)

TRANSFER the turkey to a cutting board. Remove the skin and all the bones and pull the meat from the carcass. Coarsely chop the meat.

SEASON the chopped meat with BBQ sauce. Taste it, then season with salt and pepper and taste again. Keep adding more salt, pepper, and sauce until it tastes balanced—sweet yet slightly acidic. Serve on potato buns or silver dollar corn cakes with coleslaw.

Smoked Tofu Burnt Ends

Serves 3 to 5 • **Prep Time:** 30 minutes • **Cooking Time:** 1½ hours

Burnt ends are a popular appetizer we serve made from beef brisket. For our vegetarian option, we make an adapted version using tofu.

1 (12- to 16-ounce) block firm or extra-firm tofu

1 tablespoon mustard

3 tablespoons True Made Foods Ed's Undefeated Legend Rib Rub

¼ cup True Made Foods Ed's Kansas City BBQ Sauce, plus more for serving

PREPARE a grill for indirect grilling using pecan wood chips and charcoal and preheat to 250°F.

PRESS the tofu to remove any extra moisture. Cut the tofu into roughly 1-inch squares and place them in a bowl. Add the mustard and cover all the pieces of tofu evenly. Add the dry rub and coat all sides of your tofu pieces. Carefully place the tofu pieces on the grill grate and smoke for roughly 1½ hours, or until the surface indicates your desired level of smokiness, turning the pieces occasionally to make sure they don't stick. Remove the tofu from the grill and toss in a bowl with the BBQ sauce. Return the sauce-covered tofu to the grate and cook 15 to 30 minutes more. This will allow the sauce to thicken and adhere nicely to the tofu. Serve the tofu burnt ends with extra BBQ sauce.

Washtub Fish Stew

Serves 6 • **Prep Time:** 10 minutes • **Cooking Time:** 25 minutes

Washtub fish stew is a traditional fish stew made in the coastal regions of Eastern North Carolina along the Neuse River. Washtubs were multipurpose for many families in North Carolina. The same tubs that were used for washing were also used for bathing, communion, and cooking. I have fond memories of seeing Black women cooking fish stews over wood fires in the back of the house. Nothing was wasted; fresh fish, farm-raised eggs, onions, tomatoes, and fatback or bacon from the smokehouse would all go in the pot. Those fish stews fed the entire family.

1 pound thick-cut bacon, chopped into ¼-inch pieces

1 yellow onion, thinly sliced

1 (6-ounce) can tomato paste

2 tablespoons red pepper flakes

1 tablespoon Old Bay seasoning

2 cups water

2 medium red potatoes, sliced into medium-thick rounds

2 bay leaves

3 large striped bass or flounder fillets, skin removed, scaled, and cut into large pieces

Salt and freshly ground black pepper

1 pint garden cherry tomatoes, halved

8 medium-sized eggs

Green onions, chopped, for garnish

Good white bread, for serving

IN a large cast-iron pot, cook the bacon on a smoker or on the stovetop over medium heat until crispy and golden brown. Add the onion and cook until softened. Add the tomato paste, red pepper flakes, and a dash of Old Bay. Add the water, potatoes, and bay leaves. Bring to a boil and cook for 8 minutes, or until the potatoes are fork-tender. Add the fish fillets and cover the pot. Cook for 7 minutes. Do not stir. Add remaining Old Bay, salt and pepper to taste, and the cherry tomatoes. When the stew begins to simmer, add the eggs one by one in a single layer over the top. Cook the eggs for 8 minutes until they are medium-set. As soon as the eggs are done, use a large ladle to portion out the stew. Garnish with green onions and serve with a good white bread.

Willie's Country Smoked Carolina Porgy

Serves 2 to 3 • **Prep Time:** 20 minutes • **Cooking Time:** 45 minutes

RYAN MITCHELL, Ed Mitchell's son

Fishing was my grandfather's favorite hobby. When I was young, I would go fishing with him in Morehead City and Wilmington, North Carolina, and on the James River in Virginia. I still remember the first fishing pole he bought me like it was yesterday. I appreciate that so much now. Fishing together built a strong bond between us.

As our family supermarket became more of a passion for him, he would have talks with me about becoming a businessman. He would say, "The one thing I can give you is a good last name. A good last name is more valuable than money." Your name was your credit score.

1 (4- to 6-pound) whole red porgy or red snapper (use sea mullet or black drum as a substitute)

2 tablespoons olive oil

1 teaspoon salt

1 teaspoon freshly ground black pepper

1 teaspoon smoked paprika

4 slices lime

2 slices orange

3 sprigs thyme

5 sprigs oregano

4 garlic cloves, smashed and peeled

2 slices red onion

PREPARE a grill for indirect grilling using the 70/30 method, 70 percent hickory wood and 30 percent charcoal. Preheat the grill is 250°F.

LIGHTLY brush the entire fish with olive oil. Rub the salt, pepper, and paprika over the whole fish, inside and out. With a sharp knife, make a slit behind the gills at an angle down the side of the fish on each side. Stuff each slit with 2 slices of lime. Place the orange slices, thyme, oregano, and 1 clove of garlic inside the cavity of the fish.

PLACE the onion slices and 2 or 3 cloves of garlic on a cedar board, put the fish on the board, and cook with the lid closed and over indirect heat. When the fish gets to 160°F, remove it from the grill and serve.

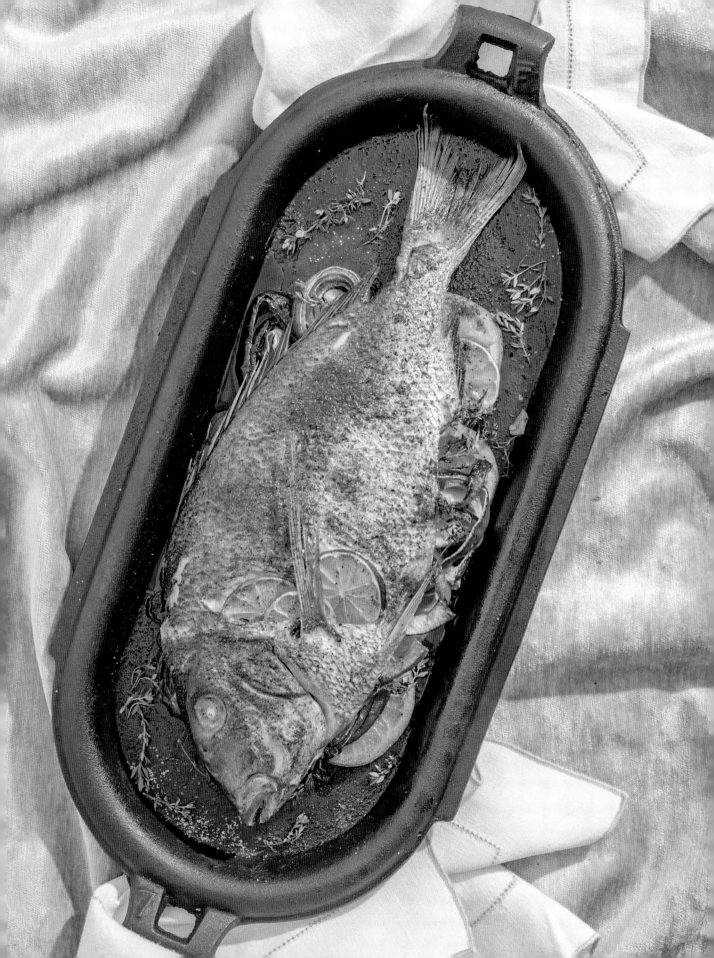

Southern Fried Fish and Home Fries

Serves 2 to 3 • **Prep Time:** 15 minutes • **Cooking Time:** 30 minutes

RYAN MITCHELL, Ed Mitchell's son

Fried fish and home fries were some of my grandfather's favorites. He liked his home fries thin, almost like chips. My granddad and anyone who wanted to accompany him would leave on Fridays to go fishing. Granddad's favorite fish to catch were trout, porgy, flounder, and croaker.

Granddad would bring his catch of the day home and my grandmother would clean the fish thoroughly, season the fillets, and fry them until they were light, crispy, and golden for Saturday dinner. Fried fish is one of my grandmother's best dishes because that is what my grandfather loved to eat after he went fishing. That was one of the few dishes that everyone came over for. The fish brought people to our home. At our restaurant, we took the time to peel fresh potatoes and fry them like my grandmother made them. Our home fries tasted like real potatoes even after they cooled to room temperature.

Canola oil, for frying

5 trout or flounder skin-on fillets

1 teaspoon garlic powder, plus more as needed

1 teaspoon onion powder

½ teaspoon salt, plus more as needed

1 cup cornmeal

1 teaspoon paprika

½ teaspoon freshly ground black pepper, plus more as needed

4 large potatoes

1 small onion, diced

1 green bell pepper, diced

1 red bell pepper, diced

1½ teaspoons red pepper flakes

HEAT oil in a cast-iron skillet over medium-high heat (use enough to fill the pan halfway) or in a deep fryer (2 cups) to around 350°F.

PAT the fish dry. Season with the garlic powder, onion powder, and salt. Put the cornmeal in a shallow dish and season with the paprika and black pepper.

Coat the fish with the cornmeal mixture. Working in batches, fry the fish in the hot oil until light golden brown. Drain the fish on paper towels.

PEEL the potatoes and thinly slice them.

IN a skillet, heat ¼ cup oil over medium heat. Add the sliced potatoes, onion, and red and green bell peppers. Season with the red pepper flakes and salt, black pepper, and garlic powder to taste and cover with a lid. Cook the potatoes for 8 to 10 minutes, until brown and crusted on the bottom, then flip. Add a little water if need be. Cook for 8 to 10 minutes more, until the potatoes are soft. Serve with the fried fish.

FISH FRY IN 1940

NEWS BUREAU
PHOTO NO. 2555

NORTH CAROLINA DEPARTMENT
OF CONSERVATION AND
DEVELOPMENT

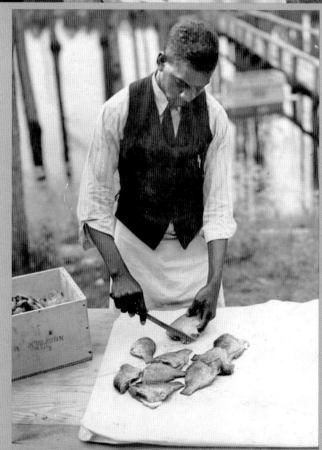

The abundance of striped mullet, red drum, porgy, speckled trout, oysters, mackerel, flounder, and a host of other saltwater and freshwater fish tells a rich history of maritime and seafaring heritage in North Carolina. North Carolina historian David S. Cecelski's book, *The Waterman's Song: Slavery and Freedom in Maritime North Carolina*, includes stories of African American saltwater fishermen in the Davis Ridge community during the nineteenth and twentieth centuries who were boatbuilders, sharpie captains, whalers, and fish house proprietors, and many who worked in the menhaden industry. "Nowhere was the magnitude of African American influence greater than along the perilous seacoast . . . slave and free black boatmen were ubiquitous on those broad waters." Today, fish fries are a staple in many North Carolina communities, especially in African American culture, where fish fries are part of familial heritage and economic sustainability.

Grandma's House Salmon Cakes

Serves 10 • **Prep Time:** 10 minutes • **Cooking Time:** 50 minutes

RYAN MITCHELL, Ed Mitchell's son

My grandmother would make the best salmon cakes. I would stuff them in biscuits and add fatback and eat them as mini burgers. This was one of my favorite dishes on the weekend. Salmon cakes or salmon croquettes have been a staple in the African American community for decades. When food was being commercialized, African Americans up north substituted fresh salmon for canned salmon to make salmon cakes. My grandmother kept the tradition alive by using fresh salmon.

1 pound fresh salmon, skinless

1 teaspoon salt

1 teaspoon garlic powder

1 teaspoon onion powder

1 red bell pepper, diced

1 medium yellow onion, diced

1 carrot, finely chopped

1 egg

3 tablespoons mayonnaise

1 cup finely chopped green onions

True Made Foods Ed's Cayenne Hot Sauce

1 cup all-purpose flour

Canola oil

Charles H. Darden Creamy Grits (page 150), for serving

PREHEAT the oven to 375°F.

PLACE the salmon in a medium baking dish and season with the salt, garlic powder, and onion powder. Bake for 25 minutes, until thoroughly cooked. Use a fork to flake the salmon, removing any skin, and set aside.

IN a medium oiled saucepan, sauté the red bell pepper, onion, and carrot until the onion is soft. Remove the pan from the burner and set aside.

PUT the flour in a shallow dish. In a medium bowl, mix the egg, mayonnaise, green onions, and a dash of hot sauce. Add the salmon and the vegetable mixture to the bowl and mix with your hands until well blended. Form the mixture into 2-inch-wide, ½-inch thick patties and dredge them in the flour. In a large skillet, heat canola oil over medium-high heat. Cook the salmon patties in batches until golden brown on each side. Serve with creamy grits and more hot sauce.

Shrimp and Grits with North Carolina Country Sausage

Serves 3 to 6 • **Prep Time:** 15 minutes • **Cooking Time:** 30 minutes

RYAN MITCHELL, Ed Mitchell's son

I didn't get into shrimp and grits until I visited my mother in Washington, DC. In the late 1980s and '90s, shrimp and grits were fashionable in DC. We didn't really have shrimp and grits in Wilson. That was a South Carolina dish made popular in trendy Black restaurants in DC and other parts of the country. We added shrimp and grits to our menu to bring that DC and South Carolina flavor. We always add North Carolina country sausage, either from a local sausage maker or the popular North Carolina country sausage brand Neese's.

1 cup stone-ground yellow grits

5 tablespoons oil

1 medium yellow onion, diced

2 or 3 garlic cloves, minced

½ cup diced green bell pepper

½ cup diced red bell pepper

½ cup diced yellow bell pepper

½ pound smoked sausage, chopped

2 teaspoons all-purpose flour or cornstarch

2 cups beef broth

1 pound shrimp, peeled and deveined

1 tablespoon Creole or Old Bay seasoning

1 teaspoon garlic powder

1 teaspoon onion powder

1 teaspoon cayenne pepper

1 teaspoon paprika

FOLLOW package directions for cooking stone-ground yellow grits.

IN a medium-sized pan, sauté the onion, garlic, and bell peppers in 1 tablespoon of oil over medium-high heat until translucent. Add the smoked sausage to the vegetables and cook for 4 to 5 minutes. Add the flour, then add the broth and simmer over low heat.

IN a large bowl, mix the shrimp, Creole seasoning, garlic powder, onion powder, cayenne, and paprika. In a separate pan, heat 4 tablespoons of the oil over medium-high heat, then add the seasoned shrimp to the warm pan and cook for 3 to 4 minutes on each side (they should be just slightly undercooked).

ADD shrimp to the pan with the broth mixture and simmer over medium heat for 5 to 8 minutes, until the shrimp are cooked thoroughly. Spoon the shrimp over grits and top with the shrimp gravy.

Dr. Joseph Henry Ward Old Wilson Oyster Stew

Serves 3 to 4 • **Prep Time:** 20 minutes • **Cooking Time:** 45 minutes

This dish is in honor of a great man, a Wilsonite, Zella Palmer's great-grandfather Dr. Joseph Henry Ward, who left Wilson as a young man. Dr. Ward was Madam C. J. Walker's personal physician and friend. Walker was a self-made millionaire who built a beauty empire in the early part of the twentieth century. A veteran like me, Dr. Ward served in World War I and was the first African American director of a VA hospital during segregation.

When we started writing this cookbook and Zella came with us to meet some of the elders in Wilson, we introduced her to Castonoble Hooks, a local historian who is treasured in our community. Castonoble took her hand, smiled, and said, "You are Dr. Joseph Henry Ward's great-granddaughter, and you are home."

This oyster stew recipe and familial memory is shared by Zella's mother, Alice Palmer: "When I was a little girl, growing up in the fifties, milk was delivered to your door and left on the front porch. It was delivered in a glass bottle. When you opened the glass bottle of milk, heavy cream would float to the top.

"My grandfather Dr. Joseph Henry Ward was always proud of his hometown, Wilson, North Carolina. It was important to him to share his boyhood memories of growing up in Wilson. He left Wilson as a young man, illiterate and penniless, and became one of the top Black surgeons in the United States. He even served as a surgeon in the 92nd Infantry Division colored regiment in France during World War I.

"My grandfather meant the world to me. When he was feeling nostalgic and missing Wilson, he would go to the seafood market in Indianapolis and buy fresh oysters. He would take the cream from the fresh milk, the fresh oysters, and churned butter and make the most delicious oyster stew. Sometimes we would talk over oyster stew—it was a special memory I have of my grandfather that only we shared.

"Looking back, I realize how brave he was and what it took for him to leave Wilson to become Dr. Joseph Henry Ward. I know my grandfather would be proud of this cookbook, these recipes from his hometown. I hope you enjoy our oyster stew as much as I did when I was a child."

2 cups freshly shucked raw oysters, with their liquor

½ cup (1 stick) unsalted butter

2 tablespoons all-purpose flour

1 cup heavy cream

1 cup milk

1 garlic clove, minced

Salt and freshly ground black pepper

Oyster crackers, for serving

True Made Foods Ed's Cayenne Hot Sauce, for serving

SEPARATE the oysters and their liquor into two separate bowls and set aside.

IN a medium pot, melt the butter over medium heat. Add the flour. Whisk lightly for 1 minute. Gradually add the cream, milk, and oyster liquor. Cook, stirring, for 5 minutes, or until the stew thickens. Add the garlic and oysters. Reduce the heat to low and simmer for 2 minutes more. Add salt and pepper to taste. Serve with oyster crackers and a dash of hot sauce.

JOSEPH HENRY WARD was born to Napoleon Hagans and Mittie Roena Ward in Wilson in 1872. As a young man, impoverished and illiterate, Ward moved to Indianapolis and worked as a stable boy for Dr. George Hasty. Dr. Hasty educated Ward and helped him attend medical school. By 1897, Ward had graduated from Physio-Medical School of Indiana and received advanced training from the Mayo Clinic. Around 1907, Ward founded Ward's Sanitarium and Nurses' Training School, one of the first hospitals in Indianapolis for African Americans during segregation. The Wards were known for hosting African American luminaries of the time such as Booker T. Washington and W. E. B. Du Bois. Ward and his wife, Zella Locklear Ward, opened their home to host the soon-to-be first self-made female American millionaire in beauty and Black hair-care products, Madam C. J. Walker. Walker gave her first beauty demonstration in the Wards' front parlor. Ward would become Madam C. J. Walker's personal physician and was a friend until her death. In 1917, Ward enlisted in the army and joined the segregated medical corps as a surgeon during World War I. When the war ended, Ward was one of only two African Americans to have reached the rank of major. By 1924, he had been appointed by then-president Calvin Coolidge as chief medical officer for a new segregated veterans hospital in Tuskegee, Alabama. By the time of his death in 1956, the VA hospital was fully integrated. Dr. Joseph Henry Ward dedicated his life to education, healthcare, and equality for all.

8

LOW ON THE HOG

Fine Dining with Anthony Bourdain

> PEOPLE ARE GENERALLY PROUD OF THEIR FOOD. A WILLINGNESS TO EAT AND DRINK WITH PEOPLE WITHOUT FEAR AND PREJUDICE . . . THEY OPEN UP TO YOU IN WAYS THAT SOMEBODY VISITING WHO IS DRIVEN BY A STORY MAY NOT GET.
>
> —Anthony Bourdain

In 2002, Anthony Bourdain reached out to us to appear on his Food Network television show, *A Cook's Tour*. At the time, we didn't realize who Anthony Bourdain was. We almost deleted his email. Anthony wanted to meet us and see our operation at Mitchell's Ribs, Bar-B-Q & Chicken in Wilson. He was a true chef and foodie. He appreciated the craftsmanship of whole-hog barbeque. He was fascinated by my pig bar idea, where we served a variety of traditional Eastern North Carolina pork dishes "from the rooter to the tooter."

Anthony was like E. F. Hutton: when he spoke, his opinion had weight in the food industry. When *A Cook's Tour* premiered, Food Network was still fairly new and Anthony Bourdain hadn't become a megastar in food entertainment yet. The Food Network launched in 1993 and per several sources boomed in popularity around 1998; *A Cook's Tour* premiered in 2002. Looking back, we were all on the cusp of spreading the gospel of whole-hog barbeque.

Anthony was intentional about meeting us and making sure that we actually cooked the authentic way. There were a lot of barbeque restaurants that had Black cooks in the kitchen, but those cooks had no equity in the restaurant and no voice in what was being served. Anthony supported Black-owned restaurants and authentic cooking before others jumped on the bandwagon. Off camera, Anthony was an even bigger light. He pulled me aside and told me, "You know, you have something outstanding here." He even took the time to tell my son, Ryan, how valuable it is to grow up learning the whole-hog-barbeque skill set. Ryan was fresh out of college and still struggling to see how our family business could be profitable, or an opportunity he would want to take over one day. Bourdain told him how much the world needs whole-hog barbeque and that one day it would be a game changer. I will never forget how much he enjoyed our pigs' feet and chitlins, and how we mixed cracklin' into whole-hog barbeque.

There was a beautiful storm coming to the South, where the barbeque traditions we once were ashamed of were becoming interesting to food media and entertainment. We greatly miss Anthony Bourdain. He was a people person, and he felt like one of the guys. He truly admired our barbeque traditions.

Pickled Pigs' Feet

Serves 5 • **Prep Time:** 20 minutes • **Cooking Time:** 2½ hours

At every corner store in mostly Black neighborhoods throughout the South, you will find pigs' feet jars on the countertop. When I was growing up, jars of pigs' feet were in everyone's barn or pantry. During hog killings, pigs' feet, tails, and ears were pickled and preserved in large jars. This was during a time when owning a refrigerator was still a luxury. We would save those pickled pigs' feet for snacks and to help us through hard times. The pickling method was a way for us to survive.

This recipe is dedicated to "Pig Foot Mary," a Mississippi Delta native who sold chitlins, corn, fried chicken, and pigs' feet from a baby carriage after migrating to Harlem in the early 1900s. "Pig Foot Mary" started selling food in Harlem in 1901. Low on the hog carried us through slavery, the Great Migration, and good and hard times in the South and the North.

8 pigs' feet

2 or 3 fresh cayenne peppers or other chile peppers

2 tablespoons salt

2 cups distilled white vinegar

BOIL the pigs' feet for 2 hours, or until fork-tender. Drain and remove any bones or excess cartilage. Put the pigs' feet in a 1-quart jar and add the cayenne peppers. In a medium bowl, mix the salt and vinegar. Pour the vinegar into the jar. Close the jar tightly and refrigerate for up to at least a week before serving. This will last for 1 month in the refrigerator.

Fried Chitlins

Serves 8 • **Prep Time:** 45 minutes • **Cooking Time:** 2 hours

RYAN MITCHELL, Ed Mitchell's son

The pungent smell of chitlins takes me back to my childhood, when I was seven years old and learned that I didn't want any part of eating chitlins. When my grandmother and aunts cleaned chitlins in the kitchen, the entire house smelled awful. My generation turned our noses up at chitlins. Not until I started working at our restaurant in Wilson did I understand how beloved chitlins are to so many. We would sell out every weekend and had to reorder ten buckets each week. As a young person, you can learn so much about the diets of those who came before you if you pay attention. Chitlins, or chitterlings, were a part of our elders' lifestyle, a remnant of a time when their small farm or backyard garden was their supermarket.

As barbeque enabled us to travel and learn more about other cultures around the world, we began to understand that chitlins are a delicacy eaten by millions of people globally. In African American culture, we only heard the story of chitlins as "slave food," the garbage of the slave master. In Africa, Asia, Latin America, and the Middle East, the intestines of various animals are a delicacy prepared in a variety of ways. Now I envision our ancestors possessing centuries of ancient knowledge, knowing not only how to survive off every part of the hog, but how to prepare and season *low on the hog* fit for a king.

STEVIE MITCHELL, youngest son of Willie and Doretha Mitchell

We were raised growing our own food. I remember the hog killings. In Wilson, women and kids cleaned the chitlins back in the day, and I was one of those kids. It didn't bother me to clean parts of the hog that we raised on family farms. When you grow your own food and feed your own animals, why wouldn't you eat chitlins? We had control over what we ate, and we fed those hogs ourselves.

5 pounds chitlins

3 cups apple cider vinegar

Salt and freshly ground black pepper

1 white onion, peeled

Vegetable oil

Hot sauce

2 cups buttermilk

2 cups all-purpose flour

2 teaspoons salt

1 teaspoon freshly ground black pepper

1 teaspoon garlic powder

1 teaspoon paprika

Vegetable oil, for frying

CLEAN the chitlins: Thoroughly clean your kitchen sink. Make sure you have a drain stopper; place it to one side of the sink. Have a large bowl ready next to the sink, too. Rinse the chitlins at least 6 times in a colander in room-temperature water in the sink. Put the stopper in the drain and fill the sink with room-temperature water. Add 2 cups of the vinegar. Let the chitlins soak in the sink for at least an hour. Begin to clean your chitlins, swishing them around in the water and vinegar. Cut the chitlin pouches in half with kitchen scissors, removing and discarding any lining or excess fat. For each chitlin, take your hand and squeeze from the top to the bottom of the chitlin, squeezing out any excess water or debris. Place each one in the bowl next to the sink as you go. When you've finished cleaning the chitlins, make sure to clean your sink again with bleach.

TRANSFER the cleaned chitlins to a large stockpot and cover with water. Add 1 tablespoon salt, 1 teaspoon pepper, and the onion. Bring to a boil over medium-high and cook for 2 hours. Drain the chitlins, rinse with cool water, and pat dry with a paper towel. Transfer to a clean large bowl and add 1 cup vinegar and water to cover. Cover and refrigerate for 4 hours. Rinse the chitlins thoroughly with cold water before frying.

BREAD and fry the chitlins: Put the buttermilk in one bowl. In another bowl, combine the flour, salt, black pepper, garlic powder, and paprika. Cut the chitlins into 1-inch pieces on a cutting board. In a large, deep cast-iron skillet, heat the oil over medium-high heat. Dredge your chitlins in the buttermilk and then in the flour. Add the chitlins to the hot oil in batches of 6. Fry until golden brown and drain on paper towels. Serve with hot sauce.

Fried Pig Ears

Serves 8 • **Prep Time:** 10 minutes • **Cooking Time:** 1 hour 20 minutes

Fried pig ears have a similar texture to calamari. I always say we will eat it all, from the rooter to the tooter. When I was growing up, we weren't eating beef from cows. Cows were too expensive and were for milk only. The hog was what was available and affordable to us.

For us, the entrails were the good part. Ain't nothing beat some good trotters (pigs' feet), pickled pig tails, a nice scoop of potato salad, some collard greens, and cornbread. That was our lifestyle; that's who we were. And when a woman got in that kitchen and did her thing, they weren't lying when they said, "The way to a man's heart is through his stomach."

My daddy loved chitlins, trotters, pig ears, and braised pig snouts. Daddy liked it fried, stewed, baked—you name it. Willie would say, "Doretha, can you make me something?" Mama would smile and tell my dad, "I'll put something together." Whatever she put together was fit for a king.

At Mitchell's, we had a pig bar to honor my parents and their generation. Customers could load up their plates with those old-fashioned dishes.

2 pig ears

1 white onion

2 cups buttermilk

2 cups all-purpose flour

2 teaspoons salt

1 teaspoon freshly ground black pepper

1 teaspoon garlic powder

1 teaspoon paprika

Vegetable oil, for frying

True Made Foods Ed's Cayenne Hot Sauce and/or True Made Foods Ed's Carolina Gold BBQ Sauce

IN a large stockpot, combine the pig ears and whole onion, add water to cover, and bring to a boil over medium high heat. Boil for 1 hour, or until the pig ears are fork-tender. Drain the pig ears in a colander and pat dry with a paper towel, removing any moisture. On a cutting board, slice the pig ears into ¼-inch-thick slices.

HEAT oil in a deep fryer to 375°F.

PUT the buttermilk in a bowl. In a separate bowl, combine the flour, salt, pepper, garlic powder, and paprika. Dredge the sliced pig ears in the buttermilk, then in the flour. Fry in the hot oil until light golden brown. Serve with hot sauce and/or BBQ sauce.

South Carolina chef BJ Dennis
prepares grits for the 2022 Black
BBQ Hall of Fame in Manning,
South Carolina

9

RICE, GRITS, AND MAC 'N' CHEESE

Celebrity Barbeque Pitmaster in the Big Apple

I AM THE DARKER BROTHER.
THEY SEND ME TO EAT IN THE KITCHEN
WHEN COMPANY COMES,
BUT I LAUGH,
AND EAT WELL,
AND GROW STRONG.
TOMORROW,
I'LL BE AT THE TABLE
WHEN COMPANY COMES.

—Langston Hughes, "I, Too"

Southern Foodways Alliance came to us in 1998. John T. Edge of Southern Foodways Alliance gave us national and international exposure by introducing us to powerful players in food media and the restaurant industry. In the 1990s, John T. and those he brought along to tell our story were the only ones talking about the legacy of Black pitmasters. No one else was talking about our story. Our own community was ashamed of our history; there were too many painful memories of slavery and sharecropping in the Jim Crow South. The elders did their best to block out those memories and focus on the success of the next generation.

In our culture, you were considered a loser if you were making barbeque. Then these guys came and let us know that we were sitting on a gold mine that had been lost and was nothing we should be ashamed of. That moment was a game changer for me and my family.

Our stories deserve to be told. John T. Edge was trying to find the origins and authenticity of barbeque. Black folks did the work—the enslaved, the cotton pickers, it was us. The culture of that time period was making barbeque. John wanted to bring back old-fashioned barbeque and put it on a national stage while advocating for small farmers to breed free-range hormone-free pigs.

It created a national firestorm. I don't think either of us realized how much of a controversy would arise from advocating for small farmers in the face of the commercial hog industry.

After the SFA barbeque symposium in 2002, some New York restaurateurs wanted to figure out how to bring our style of barbeque to the masses. In 2002, Danny Meyer and his partners created the Big Apple Barbecue Block Party, and we were among the five headliners. They wanted to launch the world's largest barbeque festival in the heart of New York City, filling up the streets near Madison Square Park. For seventeen years, we participated in the Big Apple Barbecue Block Party. The block party provided us with the biggest platform and opportunity of our professional career.

Each day at the festival, we had almost a thousand people in line ready to try Mitchell's barbeque. We had the longest line wrapped around the corner. People from all over the world, from so many different cultures, ate our barbeque and loved it! That was a professional and psychological game changer for who we were in barbeque. Back then, family, business partners, and folks from back home didn't see the value of participating in a barbeque festival thousands of miles away in New York, but I did.

Participating in the Big Apple Barbecue Block Party was a financial deficit for us, and in the years we participated, we were never offered a sponsorship deal. We had an entire team and equipment that we had to bring to New York. Although food and travel were covered, we had to stretch every dollar from those stipends for years. We held our heads high and knew that we were not only representing our family, but all those Black pitmasters who went nameless and worked for pennies in the back of the house. We were committed to being on a national and global stage in New York and to building our brand, committed to fighting for those who came before us.

Danny's team asked me if it would be all right if they brought in another guy to participate in the festival. Of course, I wanted to see more of us on the big stage. That was our introduction to young Rodney Scott. He was only allowed to cook pig snouts. We always promoted other Black pitmasters. We knew that we were stronger together. Being a Black pitmaster in New York City on a world stage less than 150 years after slavery ended was something we didn't take for granted.

Having access to a network outside of North Carolina opened doors for other business ventures, like our barbeque sauces. However, I also realize that so many profited off the authenticity I brought to barbeque. Some put their arm around me, took a picture, interviewed me, paid homage to my legacy in barbeque, and then used my name to open doors for themselves.

It never occurred to me to be careful about something as simple as a picture and an interview. I truly appreciated all the trophies, awards, and articles over the years, but I, too, had a family to feed and a community to support. The business of barbeque for Black pitmasters is often insidious and highly competitive. My hope is that future Black pitmasters receive the same financial support and publicity that other pitmasters do.

Charles H. Darden Creamy Grits

Serves 4 • **Prep Time:** 10 minutes • **Cooking Time:** 35 minutes

Charles H. Darden was born in 1854 in Greene County, North Carolina, and moved to Wilson in 1875. Darden, born into slavery, became a peanut vendor, wheelwright, and blacksmith. After the Civil War, Darden owned and operated the most successful funeral home in Wilson. He died in 1931, and on January 22, 1938, the *Wilson Daily Times* announced that the Wilson Board of Trustees had changed the name of the Wilson Negro High School to Charles H. Darden High School. The article went on to state, "The man that the high school is being named after had an ideal life. Always, after the War Between the States, Charles had it in the back of the mind that he would give his children the education that he had not received. He made up his mind that he would not only send those (9) children to high school but to college as well. And Charlie Darden did just that. He sent all his children, and there were a lot of them, to high school and then through college. All of those are today successes in their own light. Some are doctors and some are businessmen, but they will all say that they owed their success to that ideal of their father here in Wilson."

The classic 1978 African American cookbook *Spoonbread and Strawberry Wine* was written by Charles H. Darden's granddaughters Norma Jean and Carole Darden. This genealogical cookbook shared old stories and recipes from the east side of Wilson, where I am from.

In 1964, I graduated from Charles H. Darden High School. Ryan's mom, Sandra, also graduated from Darden High School, and her mom worked for Charles H. Darden Middle School for twenty years. Darden High School was the Black high school in Wilson during segregation, and it closed in the early 1970s when the schools integrated. I played football at Darden and attended Fayetteville State University on a football scholarship. All my dreams of playing football and graduating from FSU ended when I was drafted to serve in Vietnam. In honor of Charles H. Darden, our grits recipe is a Wilson nod to a few of the familial grits recipes in his granddaughters' cookbook.

4 cups water, plus more if needed

1 tablespoon salt

½ cup stone-ground yellow grits

½ cup instant white grits

¾ cup heavy cream

4 tablespoons (½ stick) salted butter

⅓ teaspoon freshly ground black pepper

1 cup shredded smoked Gouda cheese

BRING the water to a boil with salt in a medium-sized pot over medium heat. Stir in both types of grits with a whisk and reduce the heat to medium-low. Cook for 20 minutes; the grits will thicken. Whisk in the cream, butter, and pepper and simmer over low heat for 10 minutes more. If grits become too thick, thin them out with additional water. Stir in the cheese and cook for 5 minutes more. Serve warm.

Sheri's Smoked Mac 'n' Cheese

Serves 4 • **Prep Time:** 20 minutes • **Cooking Time:** 45 minutes (if baked) or 1 hour (if smoked)

RYAN MITCHELL, Ed Mitchell's son

Everyone has a macaroni and cheese memory. Mac and cheese has become as American as burgers and pie. My sister, Sheri, was the first person to bring different ideas about how to reimagine macaroni and cheese back to Wilson and to our family. Sheri was a cheese connoisseur. In the 1980s, she was hobnobbing with folks at Georgetown and Howard University in Washington, DC, and attending parties with fancy cheese boards and wine.

During the holidays, when she would come home to Wilson, she introduced us to all kinds of cheeses, pâté, and crackers that we were unfamiliar with. Sheri started to add bacon and different cheeses to our macaroni and cheese. She took it to the next level. We hadn't known that mac and cheese could be jazzed up. I didn't know there were other kinds of cheese past the ones that were available in our stores in Wilson County. I credit Sheri for creating our mac and cheese dish.

We prefer to grate our cheeses instead of buying packaged shredded cheese. Grating your own cheese will give you a creamier and more flavorful dish.

1 16-ounce box elbow noodles

Salt and freshly ground black pepper

4 tablespoons (½ stick) butter

2 tablespoons all-purpose flour

2 cups milk

1 teaspoon onion powder

1 teaspoon garlic powder

1 cup freshly shredded extra-sharp cheddar cheese

1 cup heavy cream

1 cup freshly shredded smoked Gouda cheese

1 cup freshly shredded aged cheddar or North Carolina hoop cheese

1 egg, beaten

1 cup freshly shredded mozzarella cheese

1 cup freshly shredded Colby Jack cheese

COOK the elbow noodles in boiling water with 1 teaspoon salt for 8 minutes, or until al dente. Drain and place in a casserole or baking dish. Season with a sprinkle each of salt and pepper.

IN a medium-sized pot, melt the butter on low heat, then whisk in the flour. Add the milk and stir until it starts to thicken. Add the onion powder and garlic powder. Add the cheddar and ½ cup of the cream. Stir until smooth. Add the Gouda and remaining ½ cup cream. Stir until smooth.

MIX the beaten egg and mozzarella in with the elbow noodles, then pour the cheese sauce over the noodles. Top evenly with the Colby Jack. Cook the macaroni and cheese on a smoker for 45 minutes or bake at 350°F until golden brown and bubbling, about 30 minutes. Turn on the broiler and broil the macaroni and cheese for 3 minutes. Do not leave your macaroni and cheese unattended when you turn on the broiler; the cheese will caramelize quickly.

Perfect Every Time Steamed White Rice

Serves 4 • **Prep Time:** 6 minutes • **Cooking Time:** 20 minutes

The art of growing rice and making rice dishes is ancient. Our enslaved ancestors brought to this country their knowledge of cultivating rice. Mama always made the fluffiest and most perfect rice. We ate it with pork chops or chicken or with gravy. Rice and gravy was a staple in our household. It is so important to wash and drain your rice before you cook it and to make sure that you have the right amount of water added to the pot.

2 cups uncooked short-grain white rice

2 tablespoons vegetable oil

3 cups water

1 chicken bouillon cube

Doretha's Gravy (page 77), Doretha's Fried Chicken (page 109), and Classic Skillet Cornbread (page 89), for serving

RINSE the rice in a colander until all the rice milk disappears and the water is clear. Remove any debris. In a medium pot, heat the oil and rinsed rice over medium-low heat. Fry the rice in the oil until the rice is golden and sticks to the bottom of the pot. Add the water and bouillon cube. Bring the water to a boil, then lower the heat to medium-low, cover, and cook for 8 minutes, or until the water has absorbed. Uncover the pot and let cool for 5 minutes, then serve with gravy, fried chicken, and cornbread.

10

VEGETABLES

Black Farmers and the Land

RYAN MITCHELL, Ed Mitchell's son

My grandmother and my aunts were always grilling, roasting, and finding unique ways to serve us the vegetables they grew. We didn't eat pork and chicken every day. We ate them perhaps once a week, and seafood every weekend. On any Saturday in Wilson, Black churches or community groups sell fish plates. Food is so integral to our culture, family, faith, and legacy.

At my grandmother's house, no matter who would come over for breakfast, she would have ten pancakes ready, a mountain of eggs, and slabs of bacon on platters ready to serve. Only two people could be coming over, yet she cooked for ten. It didn't matter if it was breakfast, lunch, or dinner. If company was coming over, she would say, "You never know who else might come over." My grandmother had three boys, a husband, and grandchildren who worked daily, went to school, or were at church or football practice. Those big meals carried us through the day.

In my grandmother's, Dad's, and uncles' days, sharecropping and working in the tobacco fields was a hard life. Food was available based on what you grew or what your neighbors could sell. The commercialization of the food industry and the introduction of the supermarket changed that.

Imagine the psychology of my grandparents' generation when the supermarket opened. I'm sure they said, "I don't have to labor as hard as I used to, killing chickens and waiting for vegetables to grow. I can just go and buy whatever I need in one place." Occasionally, my grandmother shops at the supermarket, but she only buys the bare necessities; she still grows vegetables in her garden and is very picky about what she buys from the grocery store. Through her, I have learned so much about the food we eat and how her generation was truly connected to the land. I admire her conviction to maintain that connection to the land. Unfortunately, my generation is totally dependent on commercialized food from the supermarket. It's sad.

In Eastern North Carolina and other parts of the South, cooking a whole hog could feed two hundred people, and vegetables would stretch our meals and feed all our family members. In North Carolina, and many parts of the South, we eat all kinds of vegetables, from rutabagas to green beans. When my dad took over my grandparents' supermarket and turned it into a restaurant, it was my grandmother who made sure that we offered all the vegetable side dishes we grew up eating. We can't abandon our history and relationship to the land.

TODAY, there are fewer than fifty thousand Black farmers nationwide, in comparison to one million Black farmers in 1920. Since 1992, there has been a 64 percent decline in the number of Black farmers in North Carolina. Slavery, Jim Crow, the Great Migration, climate change, inequitable local and governmental laws and policies, land grabbing, and countless other challenges encountered by Black farmers have greatly impacted landownership and autonomy. Out of 46,000 farms in North Carolina, only 3 percent are Black owned. In an effort to support Black farmers in North Carolina, young Black entrepreneurs including Moses Ochola, a Durham native with Kenyan parents, cofounded the Black Farmers' Market to support local Black farmers. Retired NFL player Jason Brown purchased 2,000 acres to operate First Fruits Farm, a family-operated farm in Louisburg, North Carolina, where all the crops feed underserved communities and support local food banks. One of the most impressive projects from Black entrepreneurs advocating for Black farmers is called Tall Grass Food Box, founded by Gabrielle E. W. Carter, Derrick Beasley, and Gerald Harris. Through social media, word of mouth, and newsletters, customers can order custom-made locally harvested food boxes servicing the Triangle, Raleigh, Durham, Apex, and Chapel Hill.

VEGETABLES

Hellwig Raleigh Country Club Tomato Pie

Serves 6 • **Prep Time:** 20 minutes • **Cooking Time:** 55 minutes

Tomato pie is a country boy's lasagna. Many North Carolinians have fond memories of growing up in the country and eating tomato pie. When we offered tomato pie on our menu, so many of our customers thanked us for bringing it back.

1 (9-inch) pie crust

½ teaspoon kosher salt, plus more as needed

4 or 5 farmer's market heirloom tomatoes: 3 or 4 chopped (3 cups), 1 thinly sliced

½ cup minced yellow onion

¼ cup fresh basil leaves, sliced

2 cups grated cheese (a combination of sharp cheddar and Gouda)

½ cup mayonnaise

1 teaspoon True Made Foods Ed's Cayenne Hot Sauce, or more to taste

½ teaspoon brown sugar

Freshly ground black pepper

½ cup seasoned bread crumbs

PREHEAT your oven to 350°F. Bake the pie crust for 8 to 10 minutes (a little longer for a frozen pie crust), until lightly golden. Remove from the oven; keep the oven on.

LIGHTLY salt the chopped tomatoes and set them in a colander over a bowl to drain while you are baking the crust. Drain as much moisture as you can out of the tomatoes, then dab excess liquid with a paper towel.

SPREAD a layer of the onion over the bottom of the prebaked pie crust once the crust has cooled for 5 minutes. Spread the drained chopped tomatoes over the onion. Sprinkle the basil over the tomatoes. In a medium bowl, mix the cheese, mayonnaise, hot sauce, brown sugar, and a sprinkle of pepper. Spread the cheese mixture over the tomatoes. Bake the pie for 40 minutes, then remove it from the oven and top it with the tomato slices. Sprinkle with the bread crumbs and bake for 5 minutes more, or until the bread crumbs toast. Cool for 5 minutes before serving.

Church Ladies' Candied Yams

Serves 3 or 4 • **Prep Time:** 15 minutes • **Cooking Time:** 30 minutes

Yams grew in abundance in Wilson County, and candied yams were and are still a staple dish. Every church or fundraiser plate serves collard greens, candied yams, and boiled potatoes. Yams or sweet potatoes were an affordable way to feed many, and were grown by many of Wilson's Black farmers, including my granddaddy.

For me, yams are like whole-hog barbeque: you can feed an entire family and community on a budget with yams, and there are so many ways to prepare them. Yams or sweet potatoes are so integral to African American culture. No one prepares yams as good as church ladies in our culture—with the perfect balance of sweetness and spices without losing the flavor and texture. Those women were truly culinary artists.

4 large or 5 medium yams

⅔ cup water

¾ cup (1½ sticks) salted butter

1 cup packed light brown sugar

½ cup granulated sugar

2 teaspoons ground cinnamon

½ teaspoon freshly ground nutmeg

½ teaspoon ground allspice

1 tablespoon honey

1 teaspoon pure vanilla extract

PREHEAT the oven to 350°F.

PEEL the yams and slice them ½ inch thick or cut them into ½-inch cubes. Place the yams in a medium baking dish with ⅓ cup of the water. In a medium pan, melt the butter over medium heat, then add the brown sugar, granulated sugar, cinnamon, nutmeg, allspice, and honey. Stir, then bring to a bubble. Add the remaining ⅓ cup water and the vanilla, then pour the liquid mixture over the yams. Bake for 30 minutes, then remove from the oven and baste the candied yams with their own juices. Bake for 20 minutes more. Let cool for 5 minutes, then serve warm.

PORTO RICAN YAMS
IN 1943

CHADBURN,
NORTH CAROLINA

NEWS BUREAU
PHOTO NO. 3394

NORTH CAROLINA DEPARTMENT OF
CONSERVATION AND DEVELOPMENT

During the 1940s and 1950s, a new brand of sweet potatoes was introduced to the South called the *Louisiana Porto Rican Yam* or *Porto Rican Sweet Potato*. A hybrid sweet potato was developed that had a higher yield and longer storage time. Advertisements of Louisiana Porto Rican Yams often used stereotypical images of African Americans to promote sales. The US agricultural sector also began to recruit Puerto Rican and Bahamian farm laborers to work on farms in the South to replace a growing shortage of African American sharecroppers who migrated to northern cities in search of better wages and relief from the Jim Crow South.

Garlic Brussels Sprouts

Serves 3 to 5 • **Prep Time:** 15 minutes • **Cooking Time:** 20 minutes

MAMA MITCHELL, DORETHA MITCHELL, 91 years old

Store-bought vegetables and fruit don't taste like what we grew up eating. I do buy some of my vegetables from the supermarket when I have to, but I make sure that it is from a good grocery store. I like cabbage, collards, mustard greens, fresh string beans, and lots of garlic. Garlic is good. It kills parasites. I do my best to grow my own vegetables at home when I can.

My Brussels sprouts are the truth. Caramelized with molasses, bacon, and minced garlic, and seasoned with love. I miss how vegetables and fruits tasted back in the day.

2 pounds Brussels sprouts, trimmed and halved

3 tablespoons olive oil

2 or 3 garlic cloves, minced

1 teaspoon salt

½ teaspoon freshly ground black pepper

2 tablespoons molasses, for drizzling

1 cup crumbled cooked thick-cut bacon (optional)

PREHEAT the oven to 400°F.

IN a large bowl, mix the Brussels sprouts, olive oil, garlic, salt, and pepper. Place the Brussels sprouts on a baking sheet and roast for 20 minutes, or until tender. Drizzle with molasses, add crispy bacon crumbles, if you like, and serve.

Wilson County Collards

Serves 6 • **Prep Time:** 25 minutes • **Cooking Time:** 2 hours

Collard greens are a superfood and a survival vegetable. When I was a child, Black women in Wilson looked forward to getting up on Saturday morning to go and pick their collards and wash them in preparation for Sunday dinner. Collards were a daily green for us because we always had access to a collard patch. Growing up, Mama and my aunties would come back to the house with big trash bags of freshly picked collards from friends' and relatives' gardens or farms. I learned my cooking skills from my mother. The skills she taught me propelled me to where I am today. I can cook a pot of collards that will make your tongue slap your head off. I understand now how we survived slavery and Jim Crow because of the skill set of the Black woman—they made sure we were fed and loved.

4 cups hot water

1 cup chicken broth

1 pound smoked ham hocks

3 tablespoons apple cider vinegar

2 tablespoons whole black peppercorns

3 pounds collard greens, leaves stemmed and cut into 2-inch pieces

2 teaspoons salt

1 teaspoon red pepper flakes

IN a large pot, combine the water, broth, ham hocks, vinegar, and peppercorns in the pot. Bring to a boil over high heat. Reduce the heat to low-medium and simmer for 1 hour. Strain the solids out of the pot and return the broth to high heat. Add the collards and return to a boil. Add two teaspoons of salt and the red pepper flakes and reduce the heat to maintain a simmer. Simmer until the greens are tender, about 1 hour, letting the greens cook slowly and adding a little water if needed to maintain the moisture. Once tender, strain and serve.

Candied Sweet Potato Soufflé

Serves 5 • **Prep Time:** 8 minutes • **Cooking Time:** 1 hour 45 minutes

RYAN MITCHELL, Ed Mitchell's son

When you own a restaurant, the holidays are your most profitable season. We always worked half days on Thanksgiving and Christmas, selling barbeque and smoked turkeys, so we could rush to make it home by 3 p.m. to enjoy some of the holiday festivities. For us, Sunday family dinner was time we cherished because we had to give up holidays in service to the community.

4 or 5 medium sweet potatoes	2 tablespoons date sugar
4 tablespoons (½ stick) unsalted butter	1 teaspoon salt
⅓ cup evaporated milk	2 eggs, separated

Topping:

4 tablespoons (½ stick) butter	¼ cup packed brown sugar
1 cup chopped pecans	1 teaspoon ground cinnamon
1 cup small marshmallows	

PREHEAT the oven to 450°F. Poke each sweet potato several times with a fork. Bake on a baking sheet for 1½ hours, or until fork-tender. Remove from the oven and aside. Lower the oven temperature to 350°F. Butter a 2- to 4-quart casserole dish.

CUT the sweet potatoes in half and scoop the insides into a large bowl. Add the butter, evaporated milk, date sugar, and salt. Let the mixture cool for 10 minutes. Beat in the egg yolks.

IN another bowl, whip the egg whites until stiff peaks form. Fold the whipped egg whites into the sweet potato mixture, then pour into the prepared casserole dish and bake for 30 minutes. Top the mixture with sliced butter, pecans, and marshmallows and sprinkle with brown sugar and ground cinnamon. Bake for 10 minutes more, or until the marshmallows are golden.

Summer Grilled Corn

Serves 6 • **Prep Time:** 5 minutes • **Cooking Time:** 15 minutes

Silver Queen was the corn of our childhood in North Carolina. It's so sweet and a beautiful light yellow. Imagine feeding hogs with Silver Queen corn and tasting the flavor of the sweet corn that you fed the hogs that you raised. Those were the best of times.

Early summer during corn-shucking season was when the moonshine and music would flow. At my granddaddy's farm, corn was the feed he used for the chickens and

hogs for the entire year. That corn turned into moonshine, cornbread, succotash, and so many other dishes. Nothing was wasted in our food ecosystem. I know there are so many other Eastern North Carolinians and Southerners who have fond memories of the old days. Growing our own food on family farms was hard work, but in comparison to our current food system, where we question how animals are treated and if food is real, I will always hold on to the memories of the old days.

6 ears farm-raised summer corn, shucked
Smoked honey butter (see page 87)
Kosher salt

PREHEAT a grill to medium-high. Place your corn on the grill and char each side for 8 to 10 minutes. Slather smoked honey butter over the grilled corn and sprinkle with salt to taste.

JESALYN KEZIAH, *member of the Lumbee Tribe of North Carolina and Community Engagement Program Officer at the UNC American Indian Center, Chapel Hill*

There has been a huge revitalization of very traditional corn varieties across the United States, especially in Indigenous communities in North Carolina. Corn grows abundantly in North Carolina. The rematriation of four corn varieties to four Indigenous tribes in Southeastern North Carolina started with Nancy Strickland Fields from the Museum of the Southeast American Indian at UNC Pembroke and Professor David S. Shields at the University of South Carolina. For hundreds of years, Indigenous tribes have been separated from our food and seeds. When I helped organize the Native Plant Symposium at the UNC American Indian Center, we had a seed swap, and some Waccamaw Siouan women brought a huge bag of their rematriated corn to share with everyone. The Waccamaw Siouan tribal land in North Carolina had been battered with hurricanes and had had a really hard growing season, but when they planted Sea Island White Flint corn, their crop withstood drought and rain. So many Indigenous communities have stories like that. Organizations like the Alliance of Native Seedkeepers, founded by Frank Cain, a Tuscarora tribal member, and his partner, Beth Roach, have built a network of seed growers and seed savers in Indigenous communities. Indigenous and African Americans' mutual heritage of being land caretakers is entrenched in the legacy of barbeque in our region. We all have stories and memories of farming, fishing, whole-hog barbeque, and caring for our land.

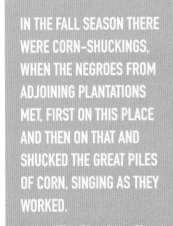

IN THE FALL SEASON THERE WERE CORN-SHUCKINGS, WHEN THE NEGROES FROM ADJOINING PLANTATIONS MET, FIRST ON THIS PLACE AND THEN ON THAT AND SHUCKED THE GREAT PILES OF CORN, SINGING AS THEY WORKED.

—*The Charlotte News,*
January 15, 1900

Fluffy Creamed Potatoes

Serves 3 to 5 • **Prep Time:** 15 minutes • **Cooking Time:** 30 minutes

At our restaurant, we always made our mashed potatoes from scratch with a handheld mixer. Mama and Ms. Paulette Morgan, her sous chef and right-hand lady, made all the side dishes for our restaurant from scratch. Ms. Paulette became the matriarch of the restaurant once Mama retired. Ms. Paulette is one of the most detail-oriented culinary queens of Wilson. For ten years, she worked for us and never missed a day. We had to make her take days off. And even when we did, she would still come in and take inventory.

1 garlic head, cut in half

Olive oil

2 tablespoons salt, plus more as needed

4 or 5 medium to large potatoes, quartered

½ cup (1 stick) salted butter

1½ teaspoons freshly ground black pepper

⅓ cup milk

½ cup heavy cream

Doretha's Gravy (page 77), for serving

PREHEAT the oven to 400°F.

CUT off the top ¼ inch of the garlic head and place the head cut-side up on a piece of aluminum foil. Drizzle with olive oil, wrap in the foil, and place in the oven. Roast for 30 minutes.

MEANWHILE, fill a large pot with water and season with 1 tablespoon salt. Bring to a medium-high boil over medium heat. Add the potatoes to the boiling water and cook for 15 to 20 minutes, until tender, lowering heat to medium-low. Drain the potatoes. In a bowl add cooked potatoes, butter, 1 tablespoon salt, and pepper.

SQUEEZE the softened roasted garlic cloves out of their skins, add to the bowl with the potatoes, and mash. Add the milk and cream and continue to mash. Use a handheld mixer to beat the mashed potatoes for 3 to 5 minutes, until fluffy. Add additional milk or cream to reach the desired thickness. Serve hot, with gravy.

GRADING POTATOES IN 1947

AURORA, BEAUFORT COUNTY

NEWS BUREAU
PHOTO NO. 6299

NORTH CAROLINA DEPARTMENT OF
CONSERVATION AND DEVELOPMENT

Up until the mid-twentieth century, growing, harvesting, and the post-production of potatoes was laborious work. Prior to the invention of mechanized potato grading machines and automatic potato planters, potatoes were either planted with a potato digger, planted with the help of a mule or horse drawn tractor, or, in some cases, hand-planted. Farm laborers lived in labor camps during peak harvest seasons where working in potato processing plants was a 24-hour per day operation. The 1960 CBS documentary *Harvest of Shame*, produced by the late Edward R. Murrow shed major light on the work conditions of American farm laborers. Today, North Carolina produces over 200 million pounds of potatoes per year which 70 percent are processed into potato-chip products.

Rooted Rutabagas

Serves 4 to 6 • **Prep Time:** 15 minutes • **Cooking Time:** 30 minutes

MAMA MITCHELL, DORETHA MITCHELL, 91 years old

My daddy would go out in the woods and get the herbs and he would get the sap from some trees and give it to us as children. I can't remember all the names anymore and I won't go out in the woods anymore, but the old folks knew how to cure with what God provided. Back then, we couldn't afford to go to the doctor; we cured ourselves.

I don't go to the doctor often because I know how to cure myself with herbs. My doctor, when I do see him, would say, "I can't believe you are ninety-one years old." I'm picky about what I eat, where I go, and who I associate with. I eat vegetables, blend my smoothies, and cook the way I was taught.

I want the reader to hear me when I say we have to come together, end the jealousy and hate with each other. When people say we ate "slave food"—I say thank God, 'cause we survived. We fished, hunted, and grew our own food, and in good times, we barbequed. We have to be honest about history; white folks learned from us, too. We were all trying to figure it out. I was there. I saw it and lived it.

1 to 2 pounds rutabaga, peeled and cubed

½ teaspoon salt, plus more as needed

⅓ cup unsalted butter

¼ teaspoon coarsely ground black pepper

1 teaspoon date sugar

PLACE the rutabaga in a large pot. Cover with water. Add the salt and bring to a boil over medium heat. Reduce the heat to low and simmer for 30 minutes, or until tender. Drain (see Note) and let cool for 10 minutes. Mash the rutabaga with a potato masher or large fork while mixing in the butter, pepper, and date sugar.

Note: Save the rutabaga juice from the pot. Rutabaga liquor tastes amazing and is nutritious!

DURING SLAVERY, African captives brought with them centuries of vast traditions and healing wisdom. Upon arrival in America, they quickly adapted to their new environment, trading with Indigenous tribes and swapping knowledge on how to survive in their new ecosystem. Eighteenth-century historical accounts reveal that an enslaved West African man given the name Onesimus by his enslaver, Reverend Cotton Mather, taught Mather how to treat smallpox, which inevitably saved generations from perishing from a life-threatening disease. In *Born in Slavery: Slave Narratives from the Federal Writers' Project, 1936–1938*, there are countless other historical accounts of root medicine being used during slavery. Knowledge spread orally from plantation cabins down through generations of families. In Michele E. Lee's book, *Working the Roots*, she interviewed rural Black and Indigenous Southern healers with knowledge of plant medicine from North Carolina, South Carolina, and Georgia. One of Lee's interviewees, Ms. Sally McCloud, born in 1910 in Scotland County, North Carolina, shared her knowledge of the medicinal properties of button grass, yellowroot, catnip, and cherry tree sap and bark to help with colds, energy, digestion, and living a long, healthy life. "This is stuff we used for a long time," McCloud said. "It's God's medicine. God made the roots. He made them and we didn't. He made them so you don't have to run to the doctor for everything."

Throughout the twentieth century, limited financial resources, segregation, and racism within the medical profession deterred many African Americans from utilizing American healthcare. African Americans in rural communities depended on community root practitioners for rootwork and treatment of common ailments.

VEGETABLE MARTHA IN 1939

NEW BERN

NEWS BUREAU
PHOTO NO. 2342

NORTH CAROLINA DEPARTMENT OF
CONSERVATION AND DEVELOPMENT

The selling of vegetables, fruit, seafood, chicken, candies, and other goods were integral to the economic survival of African American communities throughout the South, from slavery to the rise of the supermarket. Throughout coastal cities such as New Bern, Wilmington, Charleston, and New Orleans, Black street food vendors were staples of a bustling agriculture economy. Black women in particular created a thriving underground market economy that provided sustenance not only in the South but also in the North, in cities such as New York and Chicago where Black southern migrants continued to use food as a vehicle for economic liberation.

Samuel H. Vick Succotash

Serves 3 to 5 • **Prep Time:** 15 minutes • **Cooking Time:** 20 minutes

Samuel H. Vick, born in 1863 in Nash County, was the most accomplished citizen of East Wilson. In 1884, Vick graduated from Lincoln University in Pennsylvania. Vick became an educator, principal, Republican, and Freemason and was the first African American postmaster appointed in Wilson by the administration of the ninth US president, William Henry Harrison. Vick also owned a multitude of rental properties, tracts of land, a tobacco farm, and a movie theater, and was one of the founders of Calvary Presbyterian Church. In 1910, Vick hosted famed educator and political leader Booker T. Washington in Wilson. Washington, president of Tuskegee Institute and leading civil rights activist during the early part of the twentieth century, was one of the most prominent lecturers and voices of the time for Black Southerners.

In 2020, the Lane Street Project, led by Lisa Henderson, Castonoble Hooks, LaMonique Hamilton, and dedicated community members, unearthed Vick's gravestone in an effort to revitalize African American cemeteries in Wilson. In honor of Samuel H. Vick, we share our family succotash recipe, a classic dish served in many African American homes with roots in the South.

1 (16-ounce) package frozen lima beans

3 or 4 garlic cloves, minced

2 cups fresh corn kernels, or 1 (16-ounce) package frozen corn

4 slices thick-cut bacon

½ cup diced yellow onion

½ cup diced Vidalia sweet onion

1 red bell pepper, diced

1 (14.5-ounce) can diced tomatoes

4 sprigs thyme

2 teaspoons salt

1 teaspoon onion powder

1 teaspoon garlic powder

1 teaspoon freshly ground black pepper

1½ cups chicken broth

IN a medium pot, combine the lima beans, garlic, corn, and ½ cup water. Bring to a simmer over medium heat, then cook for 5 minutes. Drain the lima beans and corn in a colander and set aside.

IN a medium Dutch oven, cook the bacon over medium heat until done. Transfer the bacon to a cutting board. Drain the rendered bacon fat, reserving at least 1 tablespoon in the pot to flavor the beans and corn. Chop the bacon into ¼-inch chunks and set aside.

ADD the onions and bell pepper to the pot with the bacon fat and cook over medium heat until the vegetables are softened, about 5 minutes. Add the lima beans, corn, diced tomatoes, thyme, salt, onion powder, garlic powder, black pepper, and broth to pot. Add the cooked bacon to the pot. Bring to a simmer, then cover and cook over low-medium heat for 15 minutes.

"SUCCOTASH" is the English form of the Narragansett word *msíckquatash*, which refers to a pot of corn simmered with other ingredients. One of the earliest African American cookbooks, 1881's *What Mrs. Fisher Knows About Old Southern Cooking*, included a succotash recipe, exemplifying the interconnectedness between African Americans and Indigenous peoples of North America.

11

BEANS

Father, Son, and the Future of Barbeque

RYAN MITCHELL, Ed Mitchell's son

It was 1985. I was eight years old, sitting on a Pepsi cola crate turned upside down, helping my grandparents run the store. We sold candy, fresh meats, homemade sausages, cured hams, cheese, and other goods. Mine was the last generation to know the difference between farm-raised food prepared by Black hands versus genetically modified commercial fast food. In hindsight, I was so blessed to learn from them and to hear their wisdom every day.

My grandfather became an entrepreneur at sixty-five years old. He told me that he didn't want to die without experiencing what it felt like to call the shots and to own his own business. He worked in a factory for decades, when it was normal to call Black men out of their name. I can't imagine how he was treated every day, and how he felt having no choice but to tolerate the mistreatment in order to feed his family. I remember that he would look in the mirror in our grocery store with a broom and say, "N^%#$, go sweep this, go put that can over there," and he would laugh at himself. I remember thinking, *Damn, Granddad is* trippin'. But for him, it was therapy. He was dealing with so much post-traumatic stress from the Jim Crow era. He didn't care if he only made a dollar a day—he would never be called out of his name again.

I've been baptized in Eastern North Carolina whole-hog barbeque since I was eight years old. Barbeque traditionally is a minimalist food. We used what was available on our land and what we could grow and raise. For most Black women in Wilson, cooking farm-raised foods into nutritious meals for their families wasn't seen as a chore; it was a badge of honor for them to provide and cook with love for their children, husbands, church, and community. The kitchen was a sanctuary;

it was also how we survived as a people. Not until my generation did those social norms change.

My grandparents prepared all of us to win and to be united in faith against any obstacles that came our way. When we really began to take our style of barbeque national, we learned more about what family really means. Even though there was always a healthy amount of sibling rivalry between my dad and his younger brothers, Aubrey and Stevie, we all knew there was—and is—only one chief: my dad.

Growing up, I wanted to impress my father and uncles. It was a rite of passage as a man in our family. But my grandmother was the one who had the final say over everything. She wanted me to learn the business side before I spent more time learning to barbeque whole hogs with the men in our family. She made sure that I worked the cash register at our supermarket before I went out with the men to learn how to cook on the pits. As the eldest grandson, they were teaching me how to run a business and master the pit so that I could take over. By the time I was in my twenties and thirties, they weren't able to do all the labor they used to do when they were young. So I had to step up.

When you grow up as a child in a restaurant, especially a barbeque restaurant like my family's, you are waking up early in the morning and you are earning those sneakers you want to impress your peers with. I think a lot of children get disillusioned with running a restaurant. It's hard work. Cleaning grills, sweeping the pit, getting the coals ready, sitting at the cash register for hours on the weekend. I was tired of it at an early age and didn't see the value of our style of barbeque until we were invited to the Big Apple Barbecue Block Party.

I had my aha moment at that festival. Seeing people lined up for blocks waiting to eat our food and watching their eyes roll back in their heads in pure satisfaction with every bite blew my mind. I had to step up and help my dad and uncles. It felt like we had to feed all of New York. It was a full-circle moment for me, and I know that my grandfather would have been proud of me. Something clicked in me. I said to myself, *The line is down the street. Who is getting the hog on the pit? We have to feed all these people. It's go time.*

We weren't at those festivals for fun or to be celebrities. We were there in a place of pain. We had to take the mortgage money to pay for gas to get us out there, the light bill money to pay for help or for a hotel. There were no sponsors. All we knew was that we had to be in New York on that stage. It was a stressful time. We didn't make much money off those festivals. We received a lot of publicity, but whatever little money they gave us was just a stipend to help pay for our travel, food, and lodging. Other festival participants were sponsored. For some, this was a hobby, but to us, this was our livelihood.

This is how mainstream culture keeps its dominance over Black pitmasters. They get the $50,000 sponsorship deals, and we get small stipends that barely cover our overhead, and maybe some publicity. We didn't climb the ladder of success by winning awards and entering competitions. We got in the game from pain, hard work, and legacy. There was no social media back then where we could go viral and tell our own story, show what we do and where we come from. A $2,500 stipend barely covered a team of six, but we knew we had to participate in barbeque festivals to build our brand and clientele outside Wilson.

I want to encourage others who carry the weight of impostor syndrome. We all have to tell our stories and learn from those who came before us, or those stories will die. Learning those skills in food, beverage, and agriculture from our elders is just as important and valuable as playing ball or becoming a rapper.

Before I moved home to help with the family business, I was working as a trade analyst for Credit Suisse, a major company based in London and New York. One day, I had to move stock for a large family farm venture in North Carolina. There I was, looking at a spreadsheet of millions of dollars in dividends from their company. And at that moment, I realized how valuable the pork industry is in my birthplace. It also made me realize that only a centralized group of people profit from this industry. It never occurred to me that you could make that kind of money in North Carolina—I never saw that kind of Black wealth in Wilson. The power of pork and the influence it has in politics and finance blew my mind. Then I got laid off, and that life change helped me get back home to Wilson and start working with my dad and uncles.

Similar to what happened to my dad when his father died, I had to step up as a man.

There is someone like me in your family: educated, worked in corporate America, contemplating taking over the family business. Too many times, when my generation is handed the keys, a plague of "I'm not interested" ensues, instead of thinking, *Man, someone before me was doing something really dope. I can build upon my ancestors' dreams*. I guarantee you have an uncle, father, or grandmother who did something

dope back in the day to create financial freedom and generational wealth.

My grandparents and great-grandparents taught their kids to get out of the fields, leave the South, and get an education. Of course, that was well intentioned, but we also abandoned a lot of our skills because we didn't see their value or how they could make money. Every time I talk to small Black farmers or restaurateurs, they ask me to motivate their sons to take over the business. Far too many times, the younger generation doesn't see the value in it, especially in the age of social media, but they are sitting on generational wealth.

The mindset that working on farms or cooking food is not a viable business needs to change. No one in my generation wanted to be a farmer or a chef and have to work for what we considered "slave wages." It's understandable: my parents' and grandparents' generations, even my great-grandparents', lived in hard times, but our generation today has so many opportunities to change the narrative for all.

I do believe that the shame that used to be prevalent in our communities will disappear once we realize how others are making millions of dollars from our culture. Believe me, working for corporate America and seeing those financial sheets gave me a different perspective and clarity on the value of barbeque culture.

Barbeque will always be around, but its future will look different. Not too many people will cook the way we cook. It's too labor-intensive and costly. They will continue to invent new cookers and gadgets. I will stick with tradition and reimagine what is possible for Black pitmasters like me. We just have to make sure that we grow with it.

My hometown of Wilson was nicknamed "Wide-Awake Wilson" by the *Wilson Daily Times* in 1897 for being the center of the tobacco industry at a the time. It was a city that never slept, run by "live, wide-awake businessmen" and those with "professional pursuits." Wilsonites and tobacco farm laborers who moved to my hometown from other parts of the South worked day and night in those factories and on those tobacco farms. That hard-work ethic was ingrained in each generation.

My parents separated when I was a child, and afterward, my mother moved us to Washington, DC. I left Wilson kicking and screaming. I didn't want to go to DC. I wanted to stay with my grandparents and my dad, but I was a mama's boy, too, and I went with her. My mother made me write a letter in the fifth grade to explain why I wanted

to go home. In the letter, I explained my reasons, but the main one was to look after my dad. She saved that letter and has it to this day.

My mom made the hard choice to send me back to Wilson to make sure that my dad was relevant in my life, knowing that she and I would only have the summers together. I was my dad's only child, and she allowed me to grow up in the South in a way that grounded me instead of being raised as a latchkey kid in DC. My mother is now retired and has moved back into her parents' family home in Wilson after decades of working in downtown Washington, DC, recovering from breast cancer, and losing my sister, Sheri Hall Gilbert, to pancreatic cancer.

The women in my family saw something in me, and for that I am so grateful. If it wasn't for my beloved sister, Sheri, I wouldn't have answered the email that Anthony Bourdain sent us. Sheri graduated from Howard University and became a successful screenplay writer, a career she excelled at right up until her death. Sheri knew that Anthony Bourdain coming to Wilson to visit our restaurant would be a game changer for our family. Not a day goes by when I do not think of Sheri, my mother, and my grandmother and thank them for encouraging me to pursue barbeque as a career.

RYAN MITCHELL'S MOTHER, Sandra Gray Hall

My family didn't barbeque. My mother had five girls and she wasn't grilling anything. However, our neighbors barbequed a lot because they came from the farm. You knew everyone who barbequed in Wilson because they had the drum smoker in their backyard. I learned so much about barbeque history from Ryan's dad, Ed. I look at grilling differently after being around Ed.

I came from the more educated and upper-class part of Black Wilson. All of us were homeowners, teachers, doctors. My family had champagne taste but only had beer money. I didn't appreciate Wilson until I left. I always wanted to move away. That's what many young people from Wilson do. It is still a very rural town, and after the tobacco industry collapsed there weren't many jobs.

When I was growing up, my godmother would send for me to visit her in New York or my uncle living in Virginia would have us visit. When my godmother died when I was fourteen, it devastated me. She exposed me to so many places. My daughter, Sheri, was studying at Howard University and I wanted to help her. Every summer after

we moved to Maryland, Ryan's dad and uncles would come and bring him back to Wilson. I know I made the right decision to send Ryan to Wilson to be with his dad, grandparents, and uncles.

Ryan is a great cook. I was worried that he was going to get stuck in Wilson. I would have never thought the Mitchells would go this far with barbeque

Wilsonites knew that if you weren't going to college, you had your train or bus ticket ready to leave. We migrated to the North in my generation, to Washington, DC, or Maryland. There were a lot of us from Wilson and other parts of North Carolina who worked in DC. It was also the fear of Jim Crow that made us leave.

When Ed was arrested, I was terrified. I continued to work in DC to make sure that no matter what happened, all of us would be okay. A family can't have ten dreamers—someone has to work and keep a steady job. I always taught my children to work hard and to fight for what they believed in. I am so proud of my son, Ryan, and I continue to be proud of my daughter, Sheri, even though she is no longer here with us. I moved back to Wilson, into the home where I was born and raised. I encourage any Wilsonite to come home. It is so good to be home.

Tobacco Barn Brunswick Stew

Serves 8 • **Prep Time:** 15 minutes • **Cooking Time:** 2 hours

MAMA MITCHELL, DORETHA MITCHELL, 91 years old

I was a looper and would loop the tobacco leaves on the stick when I used to work in the tobacco factories in the 1940s and '50s. My sisters and my neighbors would get on the truck, but the tobacco factory owners would say, "Doretha, we don't want you to loop tobacco today, go and help my wife cook." My siblings and friends would be mad.

I showed the wife of the tobacco farmer how to make collard greens and butter beans with ham. I taught her step by step. They would give me food to bring back to my family. My husband would pick me up after I was done cooking and cleaning for their family. He kept his shotgun in the car. My husband just loved me and didn't want anything to happen to me. Black women didn't have many rights back then. I heard stories, but I was blessed that nothing happened to me.

His friends would say, "Why you so tight on Doretha?" and he would say, "You lost your wife, I ain't losing mine." Sometimes I can feel the sweet vibrations of my husband in my house. I could feel him.

I was a daddy's girl and I went right from Daddy's house to my husband's, and they both took good care of me. My daddy paid for his home in *cash money*. My daddy told the man who was building houses that he didn't want a big fancy house, "I just need something to stick my head in for me and my wife now that the kids are growing up." I told him, "Daddy, don't say that!" and he said, "Hush, baby." The man asked him, "What's your name?" He said, "Lawyer Sandars." The man said, "Who named you Lawyer?" With a little sass, I said, "His mama." The man looked at me and stared me down.

When Daddy pulled his money out, the man said, "Where you get all that money?" I told the man, "He didn't steal it." My daddy was more African than anything. He would tell me about Africa and he said that they had people working for them in Africa. The history of Black people ain't never been told. White folks who I worked with would

confess to me, after they spent time with me, what they were taught about Black people. It was sad what they were taught about us. I even think about how the history of Black cowboys has almost been erased from history. There were Black cowboys everywhere. I lived and saw it with my own eyes.

We are living in pearly days. It's time for us to get it right. When I used to work on the tobacco farms, I cared about my appearance, and they picked me to go into the house. I was happy about that because I didn't want all that dirt and dust in my long hair. The tobacco workers would get mad and say, "You don't have to go in their house." I wanted to get out of all that noise and dirt. When I worked in the house, they gave me great respect. Respect is earned when you give respect. You couldn't disrespect me.

Daddy taught me self-respect and how to manage money. My daddy had money in three banks in Wilson. Daddy liked to take me with him sometimes to pick cotton so I could earn my own money. He knew I was smart and he taught me how to count. I was always a go-getter. I would go in the woods and pick huckleberries. I would wash them and make them pretty to sell on the side of the road. My older sister would say, "Doretha, you work all the time and you don't have time for fun." I didn't care—I wanted to buy things and have money in my pocket. On one occasion, Daddy took me to pick cotton and I asked for the 2-pound bag. For every pound of cotton, they would pay you 50 cents. I would put the fluffy cotton at the bottom of the bag and the green bulb cotton at the top. The man tried to pay me only 50 cents. I said, "Sir, I picked two pounds of cotton. You owe me one dollar." The man said to my daddy, "Where did you get this gal from?" He paid me what he owed me and told my daddy, "This girl needs to be in school."

My daddy and my mother taught me how to count, cook, and barbeque. My daddy would dig holes in the ground, and add wood coals and poles with the tin on it when they would barbeque. When I got married, I used the stove. I would chop up the skin and add it to the barbeque. People who ate at my house always told me, "Doretha, why don't you sell your food?" So it started to give me ideas, after my husband died. At almost every pig pickin' in Eastern North Carolina or many of those old-fashioned restaurants, Brunswick stew is always served. I have fond memories of making Brunswick stew with my mother and siblings. Brunswick stew is Eastern North Carolina's gumbo. We used what we had to make a stew to feed our families.

1 pound pork neck bones

1½ cups pulled chicken (we suggest using leftover Barbeque Spatchcocked Chicken recipe)

4 cups water

1 cup baby lima beans

1 cup fresh corn kernels

4 medium potatoes, diced

1 cup okra, chopped in small pieces (tips removed)

1 cup finely diced onion

2 (4-ounce) cans tomato paste

4 tablespoons (½ stick) unsalted butter

1 teaspoon freshly ground black pepper

1 teaspoon salt

1 teaspoon dried sage

¼ cup apple cider vinegar

¼ cup True Made Foods Ed's Cayenne Hot Sauce

1 cup True Made Foods no-sugar-added ketchup

RINSE the neck bones under running water and put them in a medium-large pot. Cover with water and bring to a boil over medium heat. Remove the pork bones from the pot and strain the liquid through a fine colander. Make sure that all the bone filaments have been removed. Return the neck bones to the pot. Add the chicken, 4 cups water, lima beans, corn, potatoes, okra, onion, tomato paste, butter, pepper, salt, and sage. Cover and cook over low heat for another 45 minutes to 1 hour. Add the vinegar, hot sauce, and ketchup and simmer for 15 minutes more. Stir often during the last 30 minutes of cooking. Ladle into bowls and serve hot.

IN A 1946 *Southern Agriculturist* article titled "Promised Land for Tenants: In Carolina, a young lawyer has solved the problem of keeping sharecroppers happy," Tom Pearsall was left in charge of managing the M. C. Braswell Company plantation, a 22,000-acre tobacco, peanut, and cotton plantation at Battleboro, near Rocky Mount, North Carolina. Pearsall hired new farm managers and attempted to treat employees fairly to reduce the number of African American sharecroppers who were moving to larger cities for better working conditions and higher salaries. The article goes on to highlight the annual plantation barbeque, where "20 pigs are barbecued" and big pots are filled with "Brunswick stew and potatoes." The annual barbeque feast was held in four counties in Eastern North Carolina. This article was published to serve as a model for other tobacco plantation owners on how to keep and refine the sharecropper system so that African Americans wouldn't migrate North.

ANNUAL BARBECUE IN 1944

BRASWELL PLANTATION

NEWS BUREAU
PHOTO NO. 4652

NORTH CAROLINA DEPARTMENT OF
CONSERVATION AND DEVELOPMENT

The Braswell Plantation spanned four counties in eastern North Carolina. These photographs support articles written about the annual barbeque held at the plantation, where over twenty pigs were barbequed each year. Sharecroppers were given prizes of preserved canned foods and cash for those who made improvements on "home-making" and "farming."

Southern Baked Beans

Serves 8 • **Prep Time:** 15 minutes, plus overnight soaking • **Cooking Time:** 1 hour 45 minutes

My mother tells a story of a lady who once came to her grocery to buy some home-cooked food. The lady asked if Mama cooked with canned goods. "No, ma'am. I cook from scratch," said Mama. "The only *can* that I use is '*can* I help you.'" She always chuckles at her punch line.

My mother taught me the importance of being hospitable and cooking the natural way. However, when it comes to shortcuts, I think canned beans are the exception to the rule. Sure, if you have the time, you'll be pleased with the results of soaking and simmering dried beans. But this recipe is still delicious, and a lot faster, with the canned variety. If you use canned beans, make sure that you rinse them with water four times before cooking.

2 cups dried kidney beans or 16 ounces canned kidney beans

1 cup dried pinto beans

1 cup dried black beans

½ pound bacon, cut into small dice

1 yellow onion, finely chopped

3 tablespoons minced garlic

1 tablespoon minced fresh ginger, or 1 teaspoon ground ginger

1 green bell pepper, diced

1 teaspoon dry mustard

1 cup True Made Foods Ed's Kansas City BBQ Sauce

½ cup packed dark brown sugar, plus more if needed

⅓ cup bourbon

¼ cup light molasses (not robust or blackstrap), plus more if needed

Salt and freshly ground black pepper

Apple cider vinegar (optional)

IN a large bowl, combine the kidney, pinto, and black beans. Cover with water and refrigerate for 8 hours or overnight. Drain the water.

IN a large sauté pan, cook the bacon over medium heat until the fat has rendered, 5 to 7 minutes. Add the onion, garlic, ginger, and bell pepper and cook until soft, about 7 minutes. Stir in the dry mustard and cook for 1 to 2 minutes. Add the barbeque sauce, brown sugar, bourbon, molasses, and

drained beans and stir. Simmer for 2 hours (or bake at 350°F for 90 minutes).
If the beans are too thick, add water. Season with several big pinches each of
salt and black pepper. Taste the beans and add more salt if needed. If the beans
need acidity, add some vinegar (start with a capful), and if they need sweetness,
add a little more brown sugar or molasses.

NOTE: If you prefer, preheat the oven at 350°F and bake the beans for 1½ hours;
just be sure to use an oven-safe skillet.

Wide-Awake Butter Beans

Serves 4 • **Prep Time:** 15 minutes • **Cooking Time:** 50 minutes

Wilson was known for growing tobacco. Day and night, trucks were coming in and out of our warehouses. We had at least two warehouses, which employed so many of our neighbors and ran 24 hours a day. During the tobacco days, we developed a reputation for being a city that never sleeps. In the early 1960s, Wilson was also a stop on the Chitlin' Circuit for many African American musicians. Most liquor houses were open all night long. Factory workers leaving work at 1 a.m. or visiting musicians could play cards, get a shot of moonshine, and enjoy the night. I'm sure some of those liquor houses offered egg sandwiches for the early-morning rush and a barbeque sandwich on occasion.

Mama always used to pick up fresh lima beans from a local farmer or buy them from her favorite grocer. She would cook butter beans with pork neck bones. Back in the day, those warm, creamy butter beans kept us going to work long days and were the perfect food after a night out. Butter beans were a favorite at Mitchell's. In this recipe, we substituted a smoked turkey leg for the pork neck bones as a healthier option.

2 tablespoons olive oil

1 smoked turkey leg

1 medium yellow onion, diced

1 pound fresh lima beans

2 cups chicken broth

2 cups water

½ teaspoon salt

½ teaspoon freshly ground black pepper

IN a medium pot, heat the olive oil over medium heat. Add the smoked turkey leg and onion and sauté for 3 to 5 minutes. Add the lima beans and cover with the broth and water. Add the salt and pepper. Bring to a boil, then stir, reduce the heat to low, and cover. Simmer for about 45 minutes, stirring occasionally and checking the water level. Add more water if needed, but not too much. Serve hot.

Good-Luck Black-Eyed Peas

Serves 8 • **Prep Time:** 15 minutes • **Cooking Time:** 3 hours (to shorten time, soak the peas overnight and cook for 2 hours)

For as long as I can remember, on New Year's Day, every African American household in Wilson had a pot of black-eyed peas simmering for hours on the stove. For us, that was our New Year's memory: black-eyed peas, collards, and seafood. Good-luck beans.

1½ pounds ham hocks

4 cups water

4 tablespoons (½ stick) unsalted butter

1 medium yellow onion, diced

1 pound dried black-eyed peas

1 teaspoon salt

1 teaspoon freshly ground black pepper

1 teaspoon garlic powder

1 teaspoon smoked paprika

1 cup chicken broth, plus more if needed

Cooked white rice, for serving

Classic Skillet Cornbread (page 89), for serving

RINSE the ham hocks very well and put them in a large pot. Add enough water to fully submerge the ham hocks and cover with a lid. Bring to a boil over medium-high heat, then boil until the meat is near being tender, at least 1 hour or up to 1½ hours; pierce with a fork to check its tenderness. There should be enough water to cover the meat as it cooks; add more water as needed.

IN a medium saucepan, melt the butter over low heat. Add the onion and cook until translucent. Set aside.

ADD the black-eyed peas to the pot, along with the salt, pepper, garlic powder, and paprika. Add the sautéed onion. Stir, cover with a lid, and bring to a boil over medium-high heat. Cook, stirring occasionally and checking the pot as water begins to evaporate, until the peas become tender, creamy, and soft, 1 to 1½ hours. If the peas begin to look dry, add a cup of broth and check the bottom of the pot to make sure that they aren't sticking. Taste and adjust the seasoning if needed. Serve over white rice with cornbread.

Front Porch Snapped Green Beans

Serves 4 to 6 • **Prep Time:** 15 minutes • **Cooking Time:** 30 minutes

> WHEN THE PEOPLE SAT AROUND ON THE PORCH AND PASSED AROUND THE PICTURES OF THEIR THOUGHTS FOR THE OTHERS TO LOOK AT AND SEE, IT WAS NICE. THE FACT THAT THE THOUGHT PICTURES WERE ALWAYS CRAYON ENLARGEMENTS OF LIFE MADE IT EVEN NICER TO LISTEN TO.
>
> —Zora Neale Hurston

RYAN MITCHELL, Ed Mitchell's son

The porch is a sacred safe space for African Americans. Growing up, my aunts who moved to New York and DC never stayed at hotels when they came to visit. The act of sitting on the porch with family and friends after working nine-to-five jobs in cold cities was a treasure for them. They would sit on our porch all night long, watching who was coming down the street, laughing, gossiping, sipping on their drink of choice, and catching up. The front porch was also where so many women in Eastern North Carolina would sit and snap green beans. Food is therapeutic—snapping beans, chatting with neighbors, and enjoying a nice summer breeze on your front porch. There is nothing like it.

4 slices good bacon, cut into small pieces

1 yellow onion, diced

2 pounds fresh green beans, ends trimmed, snapped into 2-inch pieces

½ cup chicken broth

1 teaspoon kosher salt

1 teaspoon coarsely ground black pepper

1 teaspoon garlic powder

IN a cast-iron skillet or saucepan, cook the bacon over medium heat until the fat has rendered. Add the onion and cook until the onion has softened and slightly caramelized. Add the green beans, broth, salt, pepper, and garlic powder. Bring to a boil over medium heat, then reduce the heat to lower and simmer for 30 minutes.

AMERICAN AND BAHAMIAN NEGRO NORTH CAMP AND BEAN GATHERER IN 1943

HENDERSON CO.

NEWS BUREAU
PHOTO NO. 3508

NORTH CAROLINA DEPARTMENT OF
CONSERVATION AND DEVELOPMENT

As African Americans fled the South during the Great Migration in search of better paid jobs and freedom from Jim Crow laws, migrant farm workers from the Caribbean and Mexico were hired to harvest local North Carolina crops and throughout the region. The Farm Security Administration photographs by Jack Delano during the Great Depression and World War II reveal a visual history of the daily lives of migrant farmers both domestic and foreign who plowed the fields, sorted produce, and slept in dismal housing accommodations. Today, over 150,000 migrant farm laborers contribute to a $70 billion agricultural industry in North Carolina.

12

DESSERTS

Sweetness

> LOVE MAKES YOUR SOUL
> CRAWL OUT FROM ITS
> HIDING PLACE.
>
> —Zora Neale Hurston

MAMA MITCHELL, DORETHA MITCHELL, 91 years old

My mother, Beatrice, taught me how to cook. She was part Native. We lived on a farm and I stayed under my mom. Indigenous women would cook in the woods. You don't see them around Wilson anymore. My mother taught me how to cook at an early age. My parents had a lot of children to feed. I was younger than my siblings, and I learned about my mother's herbs and my daddy's. Both of my parents taught me. My mother would bake cookies out of butter that she'd churned. She made biscuits. She cooked all types of cakes and cookies shaped into animals. Women back then took pride in cooking and baking.

When I became a mother, I taught my children and grandchildren the ways of the Lord. I am not ashamed that I dedicated my kids and gave them back to Jesus. Yes, I am saved, and I pray every morning and night. The Lord has been so good to me. We are a close-knit family. When you enter my home, you will be blessed when you come in and blessed when you go out. I am a prayer warrior and I am a mother in my church. My mother would say, "Prayers don't hit the ceiling, it goes to the heavenly home and it doesn't come back void." I can proudly say that I sent my children and grandchildren to college, so I can say I went to college, too.

I stay in my lane and don't take charge unless I have to. God didn't put a weak bone in my body—I'm a strong warrior on the battlefield for the Lord. I live in righteousness every day. At my house, we sit down at the table for every meal and pray together. That's how I was raised.

I worked hard so my children wouldn't have to work hard like I did. When Estée Lauder counters came to stores in Wilson for the first time, they wouldn't sell to Black women. My employers would tell me to go to the drugstore and buy it, and the store clerk would say, "We don't have it." The woman

I worked for said, "Don't worry, Doretha, we will buy it for you." That's how much respect I had.

When my grandson Ryan was little, he would rub his feet on the floor when he ate my food. I would ask him, "Why are you rubbing your feet on the floor like that?" He would say, "'Cause it's good, Grandma." I don't eat everyone's food, 'cause not everyone is clean. Even my dishes, when I take them out of the cabinet, I wash them and rinse them before I put food on them.

301 Banana Pudding

Serves 10 • **Prep Time:** 30 minutes, plus 2 hours chilling • **Cooking Time:** 15 minutes

MAMA MITCHELL, DORETHA MITCHELL, 91 years old

North Carolina congressman G. K. Butterfield, judges, pastors, you name it—everyone ate at my house. It's good when people have faith in you. Your life speaks for itself. I am a people person. Everybody didn't like Jesus, so I don't worry about what folks have said about me. I'm too old for messy and disrespectful people. I was always taught the life you live will speak for you.

My husband has been dead for thirty years. Although I have lived as a single woman for a long time, I didn't want to remarry because I wanted my children and grandchildren to honor my husband even though he was gone.

Note: Use the yellow of the egg to thicken the banana pudding. Use the egg white for the frosting.

Banana Pudding:

¼ cup cornstarch

¾ cup sugar

6 large egg yolks

¼ teaspoon salt

1½ cups whole milk

½ cup half-and-half

½ cup mashed ripe banana (1 banana), plus 2 ripe bananas, peeled and cut into ½-inch-thick slices

2 teaspoons pure vanilla extract

1 tablespoon unsalted butter

2 cups heavy cream

Meringue:

6 large egg whites

1 cup plus 2 tablespoons sugar

½ teaspoon apple cider vinegar

1 11-ounce box Nilla wafers

MAKE the banana pudding: Whisk together the cornstarch, sugar, egg yolks, and salt in a medium bowl.

IN a medium saucepan, combine the milk, half-and-half, and mashed banana and warm over medium heat until bubbles form around the edge of the pot.

While whisking continuously, add the hot milk mixture to the egg yolk mixture ⅓ cup at a time to temper the egg. When the bowl feels warm, whisk in the remaining milk mixture. Make sure to whisk well. Return the mixture to the saucepan and cook over medium heat, whisking, until the custard thickens and boils for 2 minutes. Add the vanilla and butter and stir to combine, then strain the hot custard through a fine-mesh sieve into a large bowl. Let the pudding cool for 20 minutes before refrigerating. Stir until smooth, then press a piece of plastic wrap directly against the surface of the custard and chill in the refrigerator for 2 hours.

IN a large bowl, whip the cream until soft peaks form. Whisk one-third of the whipped cream into the chilled custard to loosen it, then gently fold in the remaining whipped cream until incorporated. Fold in the banana slices and set the pudding aside.

MAKE the meringue: Set the bowl of a stand mixer over a saucepan of simmering water. Whisk the egg whites and the sugar together in the mixer bowl until the sugar dissolves and the mixture is warm to the touch. Immediately transfer the bowl to the mixer and beat with the whisk attachment on medium-high speed until shiny, stiff peaks form. The bowl should no longer feel warm. Whisk in the vinegar.

ASSEMBLE the pudding: Preheat the broiler. Place 12 ramekins on a rimmed baking sheet. Crumble one Nilla wafer into the bottom of each ramekin. Divide the pudding evenly among the ramekins, then top with the meringue. Broil until the meringue is golden brown. Top the puddings with crumbled Nilla wafers and serve.

Oddball Carrot Cake

Serves 16 • **Prep Time:** 30 minutes • **Cooking Time:** 35 minutes

MAMA MITCHELL, DORETHA MITCHELL, 91 years old

Most bakers make use of traditional white frosting when baking a carrot cake. I like my frosting on my carrot cake yellow. I have always been an oddball. I just wanted something different, so I add yellow food coloring or a little carrot juice to turn my frosting yellow. I would walk with pride into church with my yellow-frosted carrot cake. Everyone at church would say, "Mother Mitchell, I have never seen a yellow carrot cake." I would wink at them and watch as everyone ate my oddball yellow carrot cake.

Cake:

2½ cups self-rising flour

2 teaspoons brown sugar

1½ teaspoons ground cinnamon

½ teaspoon nutmeg

½ teaspoon ground cardamom

½ teaspoon ground cloves

¼ teaspoon ground allspice

1 teaspoon baking soda

2 cups granulated sugar

1 cup vegetable oil

1 tablespoon pure vanilla extract

4 large eggs

3 cups grated carrots

½ cup chopped walnuts

1 cup chopped toasted walnuts (garnish)

Frosting:

½ cup (1 stick) unsalted butter

2 (8-ounce) packages cream cheese, softened

3½ cups confectioners' sugar

1 teaspoon pure vanilla extract

A few drops of plant-based yellow food coloring

MAKE the cake: Preheat the oven to 350°F. Line the bottoms of three 9-inch round cake pans with parchment paper cut to fit and lightly grease the parchment.

SIFT together the flour, brown sugar, cinnamon, nutmeg, cardamom, cloves, allspice, and baking soda into a medium bowl and set aside.

IN a separate medium bowl, combine the granulated sugar, oil, and vanilla and beat with an electric mixer on medium speed. Add the eggs and beat to combine. Turn the mixer to the lowest speed and add the flour mixture slowly. Fold in the carrots and walnuts by hand. Evenly pour the batter into the prepared cake pans. Bake for 30 to 40 minutes, until a toothpick inserted into the center comes out clean. Cool the cakes completely for about 10 to 15 minutes, then flip the cakes onto wire racks.

MAKE the frosting: In a small saucepan, melt the butter over medium heat. Heat until it begins to foam, then cook the butter until it turns an amber brown color. Remove the butter from the heat and chill in the refrigerator for 1 hour.

COMBINE the cooled butter and cream cheese in the bowl of your mixer and beat on high speed until the mixture begins to thicken and fluff. Lower the speed of the mixer and add the confectioners' sugar and vanilla. Beat until the sugar has been incorporated, then turn the mixer on high and continue whipping. Add a few drops of yellow food coloring and fold lightly until the frosting turns yellow.

SET one cake layer on a cake stand and spread frosting over the top using a butter knife or spatula. Repeat with a second layer, then top with the final layer and spread the remaining frosting evenly over the top and sides of the cake. Top the cake with chopped toasted walnuts, if desired.

5-Inch Heels Chocolate Cake

Serves 8 • **Prep Time:** 1 hour • **Cooking Time:** 30 minutes

MAMA MITCHELL, DORETHA MITCHELL, 91 years old

I used to stop traffic when I was a young woman. I would wear 5-inch heels and pretty dresses. I had thick thighs and long hair, and I was always clean and neat but I was never fresh. Men would slow down in their pickup trucks. I kept my sturdy pace walking. They would say I looked like a doll. Once a well-to-do man tried to pull me over. He said, "Give me your autograph, your name and number." I was married and kept walking, but he was good-looking.

Throughout my life, I have been treated with the utmost respect, but I have also respected myself. I have been blessed. One white man told me when I was young, "You don't have to work, you have the First Citizens Bank body shape." I politely told him, "I'm not a prostitute, I am married young lady, and my husband will beat you up if he hears you say that." I've always been a bold soul.

Yellow Cake:

Oil or cooking spray, for the pans

3 cups all-purpose flour, plus more for the pans

1 cup buttermilk

2 teaspoons baking powder

1 teaspoon kosher salt

½ teaspoon baking soda

1 stick of unsalted butter

2 cups granulated sugar

4 large eggs

1 teaspoon pure vanilla extract

Milk Chocolate Buttercream Frosting:

2 sticks unsalted butter

6 cups confectioners' sugar

¾ cup unsweetened cocoa powder

¼ cup milk

1 tablespoon pure vanilla extract

1 teaspoon pure almond extract

MAKE the cake: Preheat the oven to 375°F. Grease three 8-inch round cake pans with oil or lightly coat with cooking spray, then dust with flour, tapping out any excess.

COMBINE the flour, buttermilk, baking powder, salt, and baking soda in a medium bowl. Stir with a whisk to combine.

IN the bowl of a stand mixer fitted with the paddle attachment, cream the butter and granulated sugar together until smooth, light, and fluffy, 6 to 8 minutes. Combine with ingredients from the medium bowl. With an electric mixer on low speed, add the eggs, one at a time, and beat to incorporate. Stir in the vanilla.

DIVIDE the batter evenly among the prepared cake pans and bake for 20 to 25 minutes, until a toothpick inserted into the center comes out clean. The cakes should be golden brown and spring back when lightly pressed in the center. Transfer the cakes to a wire rack and let cool in the pans for 10 minutes, then turn the cakes out onto the racks and let cool completely.

MAKE the frosting: In the bowl of a stand mixer fitted with the paddle beater attachment, beat the butter, confectioners' sugar, and cocoa powder on high speed for 2 to 3 minutes. Add the milk, vanilla, and almond extract and mix until the frosting is fluffy and smooth.

TO assemble, set one cake layer on a cake stand and spread frosting over the top using a spatula or butter knife. Repeat with a second layer, then top with the final layer and spread the remaining frosting evenly over the top and sides of the cake. Serve.

"Love Is My Secret" Pie Dough

Serves 4 • **Prep Time:** 15 to 20 minutes • **Cooking Time:** 30 minutes

MAMA MITCHELL, DORETHA MITCHELL, *91 years old*

My daddy would say that God gave me a yearning spirit and I could see things before they happened. I would pray for families, even those that were sick. I remember one young lady told me that her doctor had told her she wouldn't be able to bring her pregnancy to term. I rubbed her stomach and prayed over her and that baby came out healthy and perfect. Jesus works through me. I can't do anything without him. I tell people all the time, *Be real or be still.*

I am known in my community for having the gift of anointing. One pregnant mother told her mama, "I want Mother Mitchell to anoint my baby." I got dressed in all white and went to the young mother's house. I prayed for the mother and child. When I looked at that baby and she looked at my face, I saw Jesus all over her face. Her mother said, "Mother Mitchell, look at her looking at you." She teared up and said, "I receive that." Tears came over my eyes and I thanked Jesus. Today, that child has more scholarships than you can count and shines so bright.

2 cups self-rising or all-purpose flour

1 teaspoon salt

¼ cup butter-flavored shortening

4 tablespoons (½ stick) unsalted butter

½ cup cold water

WITH an electric mixer, using a dough or flat beater attachment, mix the flour and salt. Add the shortening and butter, half at a time, and mix on low. Slowly add the cold water and mix on low. The dough is ready when it feels like new Play-Doh.

DIVIDE the dough mixture into two even mounds. Use your hands to knead the dough on a floured surface just enough so that the dough has minimal cracks. Sprinkle each mound with flour, wrap with plastic, and refrigerate for 2 hours or overnight. Roll the dough out on a floured surface with a rolling pan for pies, pastry, and other dishes.

Sweet Potato Jacks

Serves 4 • **Prep Time:** 30 minutes • **Cooking Time:** 10 minutes

I used to be fond of potato jacks, or what my mother called tater jacks. She would roll sweet potatoes with spices and fry them into a fritter or hand pie. She would also use whatever fresh fruit was available—apples, peaches, or blackberries. She would make them and we would gobble them up as soon as they came out of the fryer. I have fond memories of her potato jacks. This was a common dish for us back then in my community. Desserts always involved what we grew and what was available to us in season. We didn't add a lot of processed sugars and canned fruit. The fruit was *the* natural sugar. Sugar didn't become a thing until much later; as my mama would say, "Sugar and the doctor were a luxury for rich white folks. We grew our own food, baked our own cakes, and cured ourselves with herbs from the woods."

Mama preserved all kinds of fruit. She was using fruits and vegetables from the garden as sweeteners for everything. We never poured bags of processed sugar on our dishes. We had peach trees and scuppernong grapes, and our neighbor had apple trees. She would simmer the fruits or vegetables and make syrups to sweeten desserts or sauces.

RYAN MITCHELL, Ed Mitchell's son

My grandmother extracting the natural sugars from fruits and sweet vegetables is what gave us the idea for our barbeque sauces. In 2016, my dad fell into his first diabetic coma, and I had to rush him to the VA hospital. I was in a panic about his health. A week later, we left the hospital, and I got a text from a friend of mine asking me, "What do you think about creating a healthier alternative for barbeque sauces?" And he explained that he had spoken to a USDA representative who questioned why there aren't any minority-owned healthier-food condiment brands on major grocery store shelves. A lightbulb went on in my head, and my dad, my partners, and I then cofounded Ed Mitchell's True Made Foods.

There aren't many Black-owned natural food products on supermarket shelves. My dad is the only living, breathing barbeque pitmaster whose face is on the label of a nationally distributed barbeque sauce and who owns equity in the company. This isn't an endorsement deal. This was a huge deal for us. Our sauces and rubs are our legacy for future generations. These are the recipes that my grandmother, father, and

CHARLES M. BLOW

Walking With A Modern-Day Moses

THE Rev. William Barber II is a large man, but bent. He walks with a cane, with his helper nearby, placing each step with deliberation to make sure that his footing is sure.

For decades, Barber, who is 58, has suffered from anky-losing spondylitis, a painful form of arthritis that left him with a fused spine and conspired to cripple him, but he has objected.

Last Sunday, I spent much of the day following Barber and talking to him when I could. served the 57th anniver Ala., the day in 196 testers, including tacked in the unleashing

I walked commemo traveled to for the 50th anniversal can be chaotic. I wasn't ab river, or notice how the trees water as if they were bowing bluff rose vertically on the other castle.

Most of all, I hadn't been able to fully a had happened here: how a group of largely people in a small Southern city — there were abo residents in 1960 — gathered the gumption to battle Goliath and how they helped change the country. Bar is summoning the same energy. H hair is wavy and slicked back like that of a man rising from a baptism, and his head is tilted down so that when he looks at you, he peers out from beneath the overhang of his brow.

ks at you and talks to you, you know at his core that eludes most for his life

his mission to include what he injustices": systemic racism, devastation, the war econ- al narrative of religious na-

g for the passage of federal well as Build Back Better num wage.

er spoke at Tabernacle

uncles remember from when they were kids, before the food industry started drowning everything with processed sugar. We use zero processed sugar. We use butternut squash, carrots, and apple puree to make our sauces, stewing them down to extract their natural sugars. That ingenuity came from my grandmother's generation. They used what they had. We have five national accounts, our barbeque sauces are in six thousand grocery stores across the US, and they are available at Sprouts Farmers Market and Whole Foods.

MAMA MITCHELL, DORETHA MITCHELL, 91 years old

If I am making potato jacks, I boil the sweet potatoes until they're done. After you boil your sweet potatoes, you have to put them in the blender so the potatoes won't be stringy. You put your butter and seasoning and mix it together. Add your eggs. Roll out your dough, stuff the dough, close it, and fry it. It's one, two, three, baby.

Pie Crust:

2 cups self-rising or all-purpose flour, plus more for dusting

1 teaspoon salt

¼ cup butter-flavored shortening or lard

4 tablespoons (½ stick) unsalted butter

½ cup cold water

Sweet Potato Filling:

2 cups mashed cooked sweet potatoes (3 small sweet potatoes)

¼ cup half-and-half

2 tablespoons unsalted butter, melted

½ cup granulated sugar

¼ cup packed light brown sugar

2 tablespoons dark corn syrup

2 tablespoons cornstarch

1½ teaspoons ground cinnamon

1 teaspoon pure vanilla extract

½ teaspoon ground allspice

¼ teaspoon freshly ground nutmeg

Pinch of salt

Canola oil, for frying

MAKE the pie crust: In the bowl of a stand mixer fitted with the flat beater or dough hook attachment or in a large bowl using an electric mixer, whisk together the flour and salt on medium speed. Add the shortening and butter in small chunks. Add the water a little bit at a time and mix until a dough forms.

On a floured surface, knead the dough until smooth. Flatten it into a disc and cover with plastic wrap. Refrigerate for no more than an hour.

MAKE the filling: Combine the cooked sweet potatoes and half-and-half in a food processor and process until smooth and creamy. Transfer the sweet potatoes to a bowl and stir in the melted butter, granulated sugar, brown sugar, corn syrup, cornstarch, cinnamon, vanilla, allspice, and nutmeg until mixed thoroughly. Add the salt. Taste and adjust the sweetness and spices to taste. Cover and refrigerate for 30 minutes.

ASSEMBLE the potato jacks: Heat oil in a deep skillet over medium heat or in a deep fryer to 375°F.

DIVIDE the chilled dough into 10 equal pieces and roll each into a ball. On a floured surface, flatten each ball with a rolling pin into a 6-inch circle. Place 2 tablespoons of the filling in the center of a round of dough. Fold the dough over the filling and press the edges to seal, then crimp with a fork. Repeat to fill the remaining dough.

GENTLY place the pies into the hot oil. Fry until light golden brown, 2 to 3 minutes on each side. Remove the pies from the oil with tongs and place on a wire rack or paper towels to drain excess oil.

Note: The 1950 cookbook Favorite Recipes of North Carolina, *published by the North Carolina Department of Agriculture, includes a recipe for Mammy's Fried Pies. The recipe suggests filling the fried hand pies with "stewed dried apples," "peaches," or "apricots" and sautéing them with a "little fat." The recipe further suggests alternative fillings of "mince meat" and/or "thick jam."*

"I'll Always Love My Mama" Pecan Pie

Serves 5 • **Prep Time:** 20 minutes • **Cooking Time:** 55 minutes

Mama was cooking for wealthy white families and making all kinds of dishes: her own, and also dishes from France and other parts of Europe. They used to bus Black domestic cooks to all the plantations in North Carolina and Virginia. It must have been hard for them to see all that wealth and serve those luxurious dishes. Maybe that's why she cooked so much for us and for everyone: she wanted us to feel like her employers.

½ cup granulated sugar

½ cup packed light brown sugar

½ cup light corn syrup

3 tablespoons butter, melted

3 eggs, at room temperature, beaten

2 teaspoons pure vanilla extract

¼ cup good bourbon

2 teaspoons all-purpose flour

Pinch of salt

1½ cups chopped pecans

1 pie crust

PREHEAT the oven to 375°F.

IN a medium bowl, whisk together both sugars until combined. Whisk in the corn syrup, melted butter, beaten eggs, and vanilla until the mixture is smooth. Slowly whisk in the bourbon. Quickly whisk in the flour and salt until the mixture is smooth but somewhat thickened. Add the pecans and use a spatula to combine.

IF using, roll out one disc of pie dough, fit it into a pie dish, and use a fork to poke holes along the sides and bottom. Line the pie crust with parchment paper. Fill with pie weights, making sure the weights are evenly distributed around the pie dish. Bake the crust for 10 minutes. Carefully remove the parchment paper and pie weights, then add the pecan filling. Bake for 15 minutes, then lower the oven temperature to 350°F and bake for 30 to 40 minutes more, until the center of the pie is done. Remove the pie from the oven and allow to cool to room temperature, then serve.

Cast-Iron Pineapple Upside-Down Cake

Serves 10 • **Prep Time:** 10 minutes • **Cooking Time:** 45 minutes

Most of our daily eating traditions in the South were simple, basic ingredients or what meat or vegetable was in season. Making cakes is as Southern as it gets. Cast-iron pineapple upside-down cake was a holiday dish at the Mitchell house and then it became a highly requested item on the menu at Mitchell's BBQ restaurant in Wilson.

4 tablespoons (½ stick) salted butter, melted

1 cup packed light brown sugar

1 (20-ounce) can sliced pineapple

1 8-ounce jar maraschino cherries

1 15-ounce box "moist" yellow cake mix

3 large eggs

½ cup vegetable oil

PREHEAT the oven to 350°F.

POUR the melted butter into a 10-inch cast-iron skillet or 9-inch round nonstick cake pan and tilt the pan to cover the bottom and sides generously. Sprinkle a layer of brown sugar on top of the butter layer. Drain the canned pineapple, reserving the juice; set the juice aside. Pat the pineapple slices with a dry paper towel. Arrange the pineapple slices in one layer on top of the brown sugar until the pineapple slices cover the pan. Add halved pineapple slices around the edges of the pan. With a small spoon or melon baller, add the maraschino cherries to the centers of the pineapple slices. Set aside.

USE a flour sifter to sift the cake mix, then add the eggs and oil and use an electric mixer to combine the ingredients. The cake batter will be light, fluffy, and super moist. Add ⅓ cup of the reserved pineapple juice to the batter and stir to combine. Add the batter to the prepared pan. Bake for 45 minutes, or until a toothpick inserted into the middle comes out clean. Loosen the edges of the cake from the pan with a knife, then let cool in the pan for 5 minutes. Place the cake on a cake dish or flat plate. Flip the cake upside down over the cake pan, then invert the dish and pan together so the cake falls out of the pan onto the cake dish. Cool for 20 minutes more before serving.

Country Boy Chew Bread

Serves 8 • **Prep Time:** 10 minutes • **Cooking Time:** 15 minutes

RYAN MITCHELL, Ed Mitchell's son

We had a pecan tree at my grandmother's house. When I was growing up, she had an edible garden in her yard. When the pecans fell from the tree, they were everywhere. Pecans were our midday snack, and us kids' favorite weapon to throw at each other. In the 1980s, my friends and I would freely pick from pecan trees whenever we wanted to. It's crazy to me that today, pecan trees are almost nonexistent in the neighborhood. My grandmother always made chew bread for me and my friends. Chew bread was the Black country-boy rendition of brownies, made using simple affordable ingredients. Looking back, my grandmother and women like her made sure that our bellies were filled with simple ingredients.

2 cups all-purpose flour

3 eggs

1 cup packed dark brown sugar

3 tablespoons store-bought caramel sauce

½ teaspoon kosher salt

1 cup pecans, finely chopped

PREHEAT the oven to 375°F. Lightly brush a deep square baking pan with oil or use a nonstick pan.

SIFT the flour into a bowl. Set aside. In a medium bowl, mix the eggs and brown sugar. Transfer to a medium saucepan and heat over medium-low heat, stirring, until the sugar dissolves. Remove from the heat. Add the sifted flour, caramel, salt, and pecans. Pour the mixture into the prepared baking pan and bake for 15 minutes. Let cool in the pan, then cut into brownie-sized squares.

13

LIBATIONS

Corn Liquor, White Lightning, Hooch, Stumphole Liquor, Moonshine, and Sweet Tea

When I was growing up in the 1950s and '60s, men would sit around the pit fire singing church songs, spirituals, and the blues. We would sing, "I can't give up now." That's one song I remember. It was a time when we as men had camaraderie. It wasn't polite to drink in front of women back then. Now they are joining us by the pits. Times change. If you found someone who could make a good batch of apple brandy, it was on. We cured tobacco with oak wood. While we were working in the tobacco farms stoking the furnace for curing tobacco, we made moonshine. Tobacco and moonshine are deeply connected in Eastern North Carolina culture; cure the tobacco and make the moonshine. That was our motto after every tobacco harvest, when we knew we were going to barbeque and drink good moonshine after a long year working in the tobacco fields.

In the 1950s, my grandfather Lawyer used to make moonshine with the men and they would see who could make it best. Uncle Shug Watson would make it, and Billy and Luke Watson as well. They would find old tree stumps in the woods and hide the moonshine in the stumps. That's why they sometimes call moonshine "stumphole liquor." But they were hard on us for making moonshine and barbeque, if we thought about making money off what we created. Moonshine is still taboo.

Moonshine was a source of refreshment for us. We couldn't go to the ABC liquor store—we didn't have the funds to purchase commercial liquor—so we made our own spirits. It was a night

venture. We stayed up all night preparing a whole hog, keeping the fire and the kettles lit to make moonshine and cook the hog. If the revenue officer came and saw us and tried to shut us down, we would just try to hide it or pour it out.

Those who cooked barbeque were also the best moonshiners. It was an amazing social atmosphere to grow up in as a young boy.

My uncle played the guitar and was an excellent musician. They would tap-dance and enjoy the spirits of the moonshine. The more industrialized the city became, the less relevance moonshine had. Wilson stepped up law enforcement to stop moonshiners when my son, Ryan, was a child. But Ryan remembers attending college with friends who were moonshiners from Wallace or Clinton, and they would bring some of that good country moonshine to the dorms. It was still a form of economic hustle for us in the Carolinas, the Black underground economy. Lumberton, Fayetteville, and the Appalachian Mountains in Carolina still make moonshine in secret. Rumor has it that the mountain areas have the best moonshine.

NORTH CAROLINA has a rich moonshine culture, since Europeans brought their knowledge of whiskey, enslaved Africans brought their proficiency in making palm wine, enslaved Africans from the West Indies shared their experience in making rum, and Native Americans contributed their ancestral knowledge of corn. During America's colonial period, whiskey was often bartered for labor and was used in daily life in trade with Indigenous people. Locally made corn liquor was served at barbeques and social gatherings and used for medicinal purposes. In 1862, Congress passed the Revenue Act as a way for the government to raise money for expenses during the Civil War. The act formed the Bureau of Internal Revenue, which, among other things, imposed taxes on distilled spirits, starting with a 20-cent tax on liquor. By the end of the Civil War, Congress raised the alcohol tax to $2 per gallon. The heavy taxation led to more illegal operations and a national task force to imprison illegal moonshiners.

From the 1950s to the 1980s, Garland Bunting was one of the most well-known tax revenue agents engaged in stopping illegal moonshine operations in North Carolina. In Alec Wilkinson's 1985 book *Moonshine: A Life in Pursuit of White Liquor*, Wilkinson details accounts of both Black and white moonshiners being arrested by Bunting. On one occasion, Bunting takes Wilkinson to the home of an African American moonshiner and farmer named Cletus Joyner, whom he had once arrested. Bunting meets Cletus and his friend Bubba at the farm. During the unannounced visit, Cletus and Bubba do their best to stay calm and avoid having Bunting investigate what stumphole liquor might be hidden on the farm or in the nearby woods. Today, moonshine is still made in secrecy in North Carolina's rural counties, and has become popularized in craft culture and Southern identity.

Watermelon Sweet Tea

Serves 4 • **Prep Time:** 20 minutes

RYAN MITCHELL, Ed Mitchell's son

Watermelon was our favorite fruit around the neighborhood. Back then, watermelons had seeds in them. We didn't need a sticker to tell us it was organic. It was a given. I used to be scared of the seeds because they looked like flies to me. My grandmother would take all the seeds out and cut the watermelon into slices for us. Growing up, watermelon was a treat for us kids. Watermelon slices kept us on the front porch and out of the house. Watermelon quenched our thirst and helped us to stay full until dinner.

In Raleigh, we started to add watermelon puree to our sweet tea as a natural sugar. Sweet tea is a staple beverage in the South, and a part of our barbeque tradition. It is our most refreshing drink. Also, it is affordable and easy to make. Buying cases of soda can get expensive. But with a few tea bags and some sugar, everyone gets a cup.

1 cup sugar

2 quarts filtered water

6 tea bags (Luzianne preferred)

12 cups seeded watermelon chunks

2 tablespoons fresh lime juice

Fresh mint leaves (optional)

IN a large saucepan, combine the sugar and water and bring to a boil over medium heat. Boil until the sugar has completely dissolved and the liquid is clear. Remove from the heat, add the tea bags to the sugar water, cover, and steep for 15 minutes.

WORKING in batches, puree the watermelon chunks and lime juice in a blender or food processor. Strain and transfer to a gallon-sized pitcher. Remove the tea bags and add the tea to the pitcher. Do not add ice. Stir and pour into ice-filled glasses. Garnish each glass with 2 fresh mint leaves, if desired, and serve.

WATERMELON CUTTING IN 1945

RALEIGH, WAKE COUNTY

NEWS BUREAU
PHOTO NO. 5356

NORTH CAROLINA DEPARTMENT
OF CONSERVATION AND DEVELOPMENT

Various photographs of "Uncle Dave" are included in the State Archives of North Carolina including this image of him cutting watermelon. "Uncle Dave" appears to be a longstanding employee who worked at the Governor's Mansion in the 1940s. Historically, watermelon was used as stereotypical imagery after the Civil War to promote racist ideologies of African Americans as "lazy" and "ignorant." For newly freed African Americans, watermelon became a symbol of freedom and a vehicle for economic growth as Black farmers grew and sold watermelons. These stereotypical images of African Americans were used as advertising for other goods such as tobacco, pancake mix, sweet potatoes, and rice. Popular media including Hollywood further perpetuated these negative stereotypes.

Ed's Pineapple Whiskey Lemonade

Serves 2 • **Prep Time:** 10 minutes

Our bartenders made cocktails based on my favorite beverages and for the younger clientele we were targeting. I wanted our customers to feel like they were enjoying old-fashioned barbeque with me. We wanted to bring rural Eastern North Carolina shot house recipes to the city; these weren't overly garnished drinks. Back in the day, old-fashioned barbeque went hand in hand with homemade spirits, using what we had.

4 ounces pineapple juice

2 ounces Uncle Nearest whiskey

2 ounces fresh lemon juice

Pineapple and lemon slices, for garnish

MIX the pineapple juice, whiskey, and lemon juice in a cocktail shaker. Pour the pineapple-bourbon mixture into a mason jar over 3 ice cubes. Garnish with a slice each of fresh pineapple and lemon. Enjoy!

Ryan's New-Fashioned

Serves 2 • **Prep Time:** 10 minutes

North Carolina peaches are just as sweet as Georgia peaches, but firmer when they are in season. We add hickory chips to a cocktail smoker to infuse our peach bourbon.

2 parts D'USSÉ VSOP Cognac

¾ parts house-made peach simple syrup

3 dashes of Angostura bitters

Large-format ice cubes

Fresh sliced peach, for garnish

COMBINE the cognac, simple syrup, and bitters in a mixing glass with ice. Stir until cold. Strain into a rocks glass and set the glass inside your cocktail smoke box for 1 minute. Remove and add a large-format ice cube. Twist an orange peel over the cocktail to express the oils and garnish with the orange peel and a brandied cherry. Enjoy!

House-made peach simple syrup

2 fresh ripe peaches

1 cup date sugar

1 cup water

SLICE the peaches and add to a small saucepan. Add the sugar and water and stir. Heat to a gentle boil, stirring and smashing the peaches a bit. Reduce the heat to a simmer, cover, and cook for about 5 minutes. Remove from heat, cover, and let sit until cool. When cool, strain and keep in a container in the fridge for up to 2 weeks.

Hard Tea with Juke Joint Moonshine

Serves 8 • **Prep Time:** 10 to 15 minutes

We started offering infused moonshine to our customers as a nod to our cultural past. We had dispensers built that looked like mason jars. We had to get a special infusion permit so we could pour natural fruit purees into mason jars and fill them with moonshine. We would garnish the moonshine with peaches, oranges, blueberries, strawberries, or whatever the fruit of the day was and give them cold shots. I love sweet tea, moonshine, and fruit that is in season. At the old juke joints or shot houses, it was about the moonshine, a plate of good food, and coming together after a long day of work in the fields. This recipe is for those who need to hide a few jars around the house.

Sweet Tea Simple Syrup:

1 cup sugar

½ cup water

½ cup fresh lemon juice

5 tea bags

Moonshine:

750 ml moonshine

1 cup honey

Sweet Tea Cocktail:

1 ounce ginger ale

Lemon slices, for garnish

MAKE the simple syrup: Combine the sugar, water, and lemon juice in a saucepan. Bring to a boil over medium heat. Reduce the heat to maintain a simmer, add the tea bags, and steep for 15 minutes. Remove from the heat and let cool for 20 minutes.

MAKE the moonshine: Pour the sweet tea simple syrup into a large bowl, add the moonshine and honey, and stir to combine. Pour the moonshine into 8-ounce mason jars. Seal and store out of direct sunlight until ready to use.

MAKE the cocktail: Combine 4 ounces of the sweet tea moonshine in a glass with some ginger ale and ice. Garnish with lemon slices and enjoy.

PIG PICKIN' MENU

In 1972, North Carolina governor Bob Scott proclaimed the state of North Carolina the "Pig Pickin' Capital of the World." Scott further exclaimed that all North Carolinians had the right as "pig pickers to defend this exalted culinary title to the last bite." Pig pickin' in North Carolina is a celebration, a time for all to enjoy centuries of tradition and time spent with family and friends, rooted in our agricultural past. In our suggested menu, we include many classic Eastern North Carolina dishes from this cookbook that you will find at many pig pickin's. The Mitchell family invites you to start your own pig pickin' traditions with your loved ones, from the rooter to the tooter.

MITCHELL'S EASTERN NORTH CAROLINA OLD-FASHIONED WHOLE-HOG BARBEQUE

Doretha's Fried Chicken
109

Sheri's Smoked Mac 'n' Cheese
152

Tobacco Barn Brunswick Stew
191

Church Ladies' Candied Yams
163

Southern Baked Beans
198

Wilson County Collards
168

Fluffy Creamed Potatoes
174

Summer Grilled Corn
172

Ed's Shindig Slaw
98

Classic Skillet Cornbread
89

"I Don't Eat Everybody's Potato Salad!"
100

Watermelon Sweet Tea
233

PITMASTER
PITMASTER
RETURN BBQ TO ITS ROOTS
PITMASTER
RETURN BBQ TO ITS ROOTS
PITMASTER
PITMASTER
Ed Mitchell

Ed Mitchell's Barbeque
PLAYLIST

Available on Spotify and Apple Music

Pig pickin' is where barbeque, music, and tradition become a celebration. We wanted to share some of the Mitchell family's favorite songs, from each generation, to enjoy at your next pig pickin'. Many of these songs tell the story of American barbeque and chronicle the lives of the enslaved, sharecroppers, pitmasters, cooks, moonshiners, bluesmen, and those who left the South during the Great Migration. Barbeque and music are the soundtracks of our lives from generation to generation.

"I Can't Give Up" by Lee Williams & the Spiritual QC's

"Like a Ship" by Pastor T. L. Barrett & the Youth for Christ Choir

"Trouble Don't Last Always" by Rev. Timothy Wright

"I Am Born Again" by the Edwin Hawkins Music & Arts Seminar Mass Choir

"His Eye Is on the Sparrow" by Mahalia Jackson

"Let Us Break Bread Together" by Marian Anderson

"In the Pines" by Lead Belly

"Old Corn Likker" by Carolina Chocolate Drops

"Cornbread and Butterbeans" by Carolina Chocolate Drops

"Cloudy Sky Blues" by Barbeque Bob (Robert Hicks)

"Chocolate to the Bone" by Barbeque Bob (Robert Hicks)

"Going On Strike" by the Emotions

"Front Line" by Stevie Wonder

"I Say a Little Prayer" by Dionne Warwick

"The Makings of You" by Curtis Mayfield

"You're All I Need to Get By" by Marvin Gaye and Tammi Terrell

"Give Me Just a Little More Time" by the Chairmen of the Board

"Glad to Be Home" by Charles Smith and Jeff Cooper

"Promise That You'll Wait" by Michael Lizzmore

"I'll Be Home" by Artie Golden

"John Brown" by the Staple Singers

"What's Going On" by Marvin Gaye

"I Wish I Knew How It Felt to Be Free" by Nina Simone (Studio Rio version)

"Moonshine Blues" by Ma Rainey

"Mannish Boy" by Muddy Waters

"I'm Old Fashioned" by John Coltrane

"Struttin' with Some Barbeque" by Louis Armstrong

"Straight, No Chaser" by Thelonious Monk

"Blues for the Barbeque" by Count Basie

"Hot Barbeque" by Jack McDuff

"Stone Soul Picnic" by the Supremes and Four Tops

"Who Can I Run To" by the Jones Girls

"Jesus Will Save" by Shirley Caesar

"I Won't Be Troubled No More" by Shirley Caesar

"Best of Me" by Anthony Hamilton

"All I Do" by Stevie Wonder

"What You Won't Do for Love" by Bobby Caldwell

"Come Live with Me Angel" by Marvin Gaye

"I Got a Woman" by Ray Charles

"Corn Licker & Barbeque" by Fiddlin, John Carson

"Grandma's Hands" by Bill Withers

"Hey! Love" by the Delfonics

"Playa Hater" by the Notorious B.I.G.

"He's My Friend" by Rahni Harris & Family Love

"Fishin' Blues" by Taj Mahal

"DownHome Girl" by Betty Davis

"Tobacco Road" by Lou Rawls

"Homesong" by the Cavemen

"Greetings (This Is Uncle Sam)" by the Monitors

"Step by Step (Hand in Hand)" by the Monitors

"Bar-B-Q" by Wendy Rene

"Southern Man" by Merry Clayton

"So Fresh, So Clean" by OutKast

"Ms. Fat Booty" by Mos Def

"Family Reunion" by the Original O'Jays

"He's an On Time God" by Dottie Peoples

"Before I Let Go" by Frankie Beverly and Maze

"Happy Feelings" by Frankie Beverly and Maze

"The Makings of You" by Curtis Mayfield

"Southern Girl" by Frankie Beverly and Maze

"We Are Family" by Sister Sledge

"Pass the Peas" by the J.B.'s

"Don't Tell a Lie About Me and I Won't Tell the Truth on You" by James Brown

"Dreaming About You" by the Blackbyrds

"Summer Madness" by Kool & The Gang

"Hustler's Ambition" by 50 Cent

"Dedication" by Nipsey Hussle

"The Heart Part 5" by Kendrick Lamar

"Walkin" by Denzel Curry

"Fried Neckbones and Some Home Fries" by Willie Bobo

"Free Mind" by Tems

"Cornbread, Fish & Collard Greens" by Anthony Hamilton

"Soul Food" by Goodie Mob

"Closer" by Goapele

"Int'l Players Anthem (I Choose You)" by UGK and OutKast

"Eu Bem Que Te Avisei (Tu Empinou Ele Pei)" by MC Delux

"Até A Próxima Vida" by Gustavo Remix Oficial

"Tem Cabaré Essa Noite" by Nivaldo Marques & Nattan

"Oge" by the Cavemen

"Logba Logba" by Simi

"Wild Dreams" by Burna Boy

"God Did" by DJ Khaled

ACKNOWLEDGMENTS

Special thanks to Lisa Y. Henderson, LaMonique Hamilton, Castonoble Hooks, *Black Wide-Awake*, the Lane Project, Freeman Roundhouse Museum, Ashley Johnson; Dr. David Shields, Jesalyn Keziah, Earthen Studios, Vivian Howard, UNC Louis Round Wilson Special Collections Library, the State Archives of North Carolina, Dr. Howard Conyers, John T. Edge, and Adrian Miller.

We would also like to thank the venues that graciously hosted our photo shoots for this book—The Ponderosa, Aerie Bed & Breakfast, and The Maola at Riverside—as well as the team behind the imagery, as follows:

Baxter Miller, photographer
Ryan Stancil, producer
Ashley Johnson, recipe stylist
Kay Stancil, culinary producer
Liese Rose, retoucher

INDEX

smoking or curing leaves in, 68–69
underpayment of workers in, 70, 71
Today show, 36
Tofu Burnt Ends, Smoked, 118
tomato(es):
Bacon Jam, Hellwig, 78, *79*
Fried Green, Let 'Em Roll, 32, *33*
Pie, Hellwig Raleigh Country Club, 160, *161*
turkey, barbequed whole:
BBQ sauce for, 74
Bougie, 116–17
Turner, Helen, 6

U

Upside-Down Cake, Pineapple, Cast-Iron, 224, *225*

V

Vegetable Martha (1939), *181*
vegetables, 157–83
Candied Sweet Potato Soufflé, *170*, 171
Candied Yams, Church Ladies', *162*, 163
Collards, Wilson County, 168, *169*
Corn, Summer Grilled, 172, *172*
Garlic Brussels Sprouts, *166*, 167
growing one's own, 97, 158
Potatoes, Fluffy Creamed, 174, *175*
Rutabagas, Rooted, 178, *179*
store-bought, 158, 167, 198
Succotash, Samuel H. Vick, 182–83, *183*
Vietnam War, 92, 93
Vinegar BBQ Sauce, Eastern North Carolina, Ed's, 74, 75

W

Waccamaw Sioux, 173
Walker, Madam C. J., xviii, 130, 133
Ward, Dr. Joseph Henry, xviii, 130–32, 133
Washington, Booker T., 182
Washington Post, 29
Washtub Fish Stew, 119

watermelon:
cutting (1945), *234*
Sweet Tea, *232*, 233
Wedge Salad, Blue Cheese, with BBQ Chicken, 94, *95*
What Mrs. Fisher Knows About Old Southern Cooking, 183
Where Main Street Meets the River (Carter), 67
Whiskey Pineapple Lemonade, Ed's, 235
White Rice, Steamed, Perfect Every Time, 155
whole-hog barbeque:
above ground indoor pits for, 83
by African American vs. white entrepreneurs, 6–7
at Braswell Plantation (1944), *48–49*, 195, *196–97*
building a fire for, 9, 105
chopped style of, 74
mastering art of, with Mr. Kirby, 105–6
menu for, 241
Mitchells' Eastern North Carolina Old-Fashioned, 14–16, *15*, *17*
moonshine and, 83, 230
pig pickin' style of, 74
playlist for, 243–47
Wilkinson, Alec, 231
Wilson Daily Times, 29, 52, 150, 189
Working the Roots (Lee), 180
World War I, 130, 133

Y

yams:
Candied, Church Ladies', *162*, 163
Porto Rican (1943), *164–65*
see also sweet potato(es)
Yellow Cake, 216–17

Z

Zimmern, Andrew, 64

ABOUT THE AUTHORS

ED MITCHELL, known as "the Pitmaster" in barbeque circles, has been cooking whole-hog barbeque the traditional way since he was a teenager in Wilson, North Carolina. Thanks to a chance launch and Ed's habit-forming barbeque, Mitchell's Grocery soon morphed into Mitchell's Ribs, Chicken & Bar-B-Q. In 2009, Ed was invited to cook at the prestigious James Beard House in New York City. A year later, notable food advocate and author Michael Pollan shadowed Ed in preparation for his *New York Times* bestselling book *Cooked: A Natural History of Transformation*. Ed was not only featured in the book, but also in the Netflix original food documentary *Cooked*. The Preserve, the next Mitchell venture, will open in Raleigh, North Carolina, in the summer of 2023. Ed Mitchell enthusiasts can find his famous sauces and rubs made with zero processed sugar by True Made Foods, available at Whole Foods, Kroger, and Sprouts grocery stores nationwide. Ed Mitchell was inducted into the 2022 Black BBQ Hall of Fame and the American Royal Barbecue Hall of Fame.

RYAN MITCHELL, Ed's only son, serves as the business and technological brain behind his father's brand. Long before the Pitmaster fame, Ryan could be found by the side of his grandparents, Willie and Doretha Mitchell, at their small corner store. Although barbeque was the only way of life he knew, Ryan originally pictured a different path for this career. After high school, Ryan charted his own course and attended East Carolina University to pursue his dreams of playing college football and earn a degree in economics. He spent eight years working in commercial and investment banking for some of the nation's largest firms before he reevaluated his professional life and returned to his roots in barbeque. As the keeper of the family legacy, Ryan spends the majority of his time managing the business side of the Ed Mitchell brand. Ryan credits his father, grandfather, and uncles Aubrey and Stevie Mitchell for giving him the skills to lead the next generation of barbeque enthusiasts.

ZELLA PALMER, author, professor, filmmaker, curator, and scholar, is the chair and director of the Dillard University Ray Charles Program in African American Material Culture in New Orleans, Louisiana. Palmer filmed and produced the documentary *The Story of New Orleans Creole Cooking: The Black Hand in the Pot*. In 2020, under Palmer's leadership, Dillard University launched a food studies minor, one of two accredited academic food studies programs at a Historically Black College & University (HBCU). Palmer also is the author of *Recipes and Remembrances of Fair Dillard: 1869–2019*, archival recipes and stories from Dillard University. In 2016, she was a guest speaker at Nicholls State University and Maryville University, and for the NYU Food Studies program. Palmer's research and articles has appeared in the Louisiana Endowment for the Humanities' *64 Parishes*, *Essence*, and *For the Culture* magazine. Palmer received the 2018 Cultural Bearer Award from the Mardi Gras Indian Hall of Fame and the 2022 Dine Diaspora Black Women in Food Trailblazer honor, and was named one of the 2020 People to Watch by *New Orleans* magazine.

HarperCollins books may be purchased for educational,
business, or sales promotional use. For information,
please email the Special Markets Department at
SPsales@harpercollins.com.

Ecco® and HarperCollins® are trademarks of
HarperCollins Publishers.

FIRST EDITION

DESIGNED BY RENATA DE OLIVEIRA

Photographs by Baxter Miller

Library of Congress Cataloging-in-Publication Data
has been applied for.

ISBN 978-0-06-308838-2

23 24 25 26 27   TC   10 9 8 7 6 5 4 3 2 1